From Nanango to Cooktown

From Nanango to Cooktown

The Queensland Memoir of a Mining Warden's Daughter

1930-1955

LENNIE WALLACE

First published in 2006 by Central Queensland University Press

Second published in 2012 by Boolarong Press, Salisbury, Brisbane, Australia.

National Library of Australia Cataloguing-in-Publication entry

Author:	Wallace, Lennie.
Title:	From Nanango to Cooktown : the Queensland memoir of a miningwarden's daughter 1930-1955 / Lennie Wallace.
ISBN:	9781921920554 (pbk.)
Subjects:	Wallace, Lennie. Country life--Queensland. Queensland--Social life and customs--20th century.
Dewey Number:	994.304092

Front cover image: Red poinsiana flowers, Cooktown, 1986 Courtesy John Oxley Library

Back cover image: Coronation Hotel at Nanango, ca. 1911 Courtesy John Oxley Library

Printed and bound by Watson Ferguson & Company, Salisbury, Brisbane, Australia.

Contents

My Life Begins

I was born in October, 1930, in the little south-eastern Queensland town of Nanango, one of the first rural settlements in Queensland. It was an ideal town for a young child and I felt a warm, possessive glow when my beloved Gran told me that her father was instrumental in the European genesis of Nanango town. He was Zachariah Skyring, with business interests both in Sydney and very early Brisbane. Zac, to distinguish him from his equally esteemed son, Zach, married Rosetta Sparkes of the Brisbane butchering family. Zac, for some time, joined his in-laws in that trade and, in the early days of 1867 set off to inspect some fat sheep that were for sale on Nanango station.

After his horses were settled for the night in the stables at Bright's Burnet Inn, he met up with an ex-Victorian miner who was working as shepherd on Nanango station.[1] The shepherd knew who Zac was and that he was the man who had come to inspect the sheep in his charge but he wanted, not to talk about sheep, but to brag about a gold find that he said, 'licks Victoria into a cocked hat' To emphasise his point, he undid the top of his trousers and pulled from a hidden belt about his waist two bags of 'splendid alluvial gold'. It weighed about a kilogram and was the most eye-catching alluvial that Zac had ever seen. He had to make a quick decision of gold versus mutton. Gold won.

A daylight start was made with his new partner to the gold prospect about 5 kilometres from the inn. The miner produced a pick, shovel and gold- dish from under a bush and dirt was taken and washed from the bottom of a hole he had already started. After a day's digging, the newly-formed partnership was an ounce of gold richer. During their mining activities a 'big mob' of Aborigines came to watch, baffled as to what white-feller 'bin look out long coochee mudlo'. The old miner knew the ropes and explained that his partner, Zac, would have to return to Brisbane as soon as possible to 'secure a legal right to their gold find'. Zac saw the logic in this and, two days after leaving the camp, turned up

---

1 James Nash *Gympie Times October 16th 1917*

at the Premier's office with his gold. Premier Herbert was 'dumbstruck'[2] and straightaway escorted Zac to display his gold to the Governor. (Zac's brother, Dan, had been a member of the Governor's escort when he first arrived to take up duties in Brisbane.)

Lady Bowen and her lady companions rushed in when they heard of the find. Governor Bowen was ecstatic. The new Colony was practically bankrupt. On its secession from New South Wales it was left with only four pence halfpenny in the Treasury. This was equivalent to less than today's five cents, but, as my teacher of the late 1930s told her class, it would then (1938) buy 'a pie and a cream bun'. A decent goldrush would work wonders with the Colony's economy.

Nanango Goldfield

Zac was eagerly equipped with a Miner's Right and the partner's claim legalised. He took the gold to Flavelle's, the jeweller's shop, where he was paid a big cheque of four pounds and six pence ($8.05 in today's decimal currency). The gold was received in a fever of excitement and high expectations, heaped up in a fancy dish and displayed in the shop window with an accompanying notice *From the Nanango Goldfield.* Among the crowd of hundreds who blocked the sidewalk to admire the gold were three miners just arrived down from the Calliope field near Gladstone. They immediately sent word to their mates and the 'move swept Gladstone of every sign of habitation'[3] Among the four hundred miners who packed their gear and left, was James Nash, an acquaintance – and later a relative by marriage – of Zac's.

The Nanango goldfield didn't live up to the lofty expectations of the miners. James Nash, always a solitary miner who worked by choice on his own, saw the field's short-comings, packed his gear and quietly left. He made his way, following a barely-defined track, to Maryborough. He intended to try his luck again at Calliope but changed his mind and went to Brisbane where he purchased a horse and rations with the last of his money and set out to return to Maryborough. On the way, he met up with other prospectors and they washed a few dishes of gold in likely-looking gullies along the way.

Before he reached Maryborough, he camped on a gully later to become famous as 'Nash's Gully'. There was a small waterhole there and after lighting a fire and putting the billy on to boil, Nash decided to try a prospect. Before he'd finished washing his first dish he spotted the heart-warming gleam of first one nugget and then another. He tried a little longer with similar happy results. As soon as he'd eaten his meal, he 'covered all traces of his fire' and went to make

2 James Nash *Gympie Times October 16th 1917*

3 James Nash *Gympie Times October 16th 1917*

camp some distance away. At daylight next morning he went higher up the gully and, from a drive in the bank, got more gold. Then catastrophe struck. He broke his miner's pick. Unable to work without it, he hurried on to Maryborough. He 'tried two banks and several stores' but times were so bad, no one wanted to buy anything as frivolous as gold. Eventually, Southerden, a store-keeper, gave him a pound ($2) in cash and another two pounds worth of tools and tucker.

Nash returned to the gully and obtained more and more gold. In six days he found 74 ounces, then worth three pounds an ounce in Brisbane, now worth at least $30,000. Covering his tracks at the mine first, he made his way back to Maryborough and paid his steamer fare to Brisbane with one of the nuggets, then went, like Zac, to Flavelle's where he sold his gold for 200 pounds ($400, in those days a not-too-small fortune). A Member of Parliament with some knowledge of mining, W.H.Walsh, the member for Maryborough, was in the shop at the time and asked where Nash had found the gold. Anxious not to give the show away, Nash just answered, 'Oh, up north'. Naturally, his find created a lot of interest and curiosity so Nash tried to give the impression that the gold had been found over a lengthy period of prospecting and not just from one golden gully not that far north of Brisbane. He kept up this discretionary evasion until he was joined by his brother John. On 16th October 1867, Nash reported to Sergeant Ware his discovery of gold at Gympie Creek and legalised the brothers' claim.

Next day, the *Brisbane Courier* contained a news item from Maryborough[4], 'Two brothers named Nash came to town yesterday and reported a find of gold weighed 75 ounces on the Mary River at Widgee Crossing'. Gympie's gold rush was on. Nash duly received a reward and Queensland was saved from bankruptcy.

Light Horse Days

My mother and father both grew up in Gympie, though my father was actually born in Charters Towers while his father was working at the Black Jack mine there. They knew each other during their childhood and married a few years after the end of World War 1 when my father, Jack Waddell, gained a secure job in the Public Service as Mining Warden's clerk in Chillagoe. Both he and his older brother, George, had served in the 2nd Light Horse in the Middle East. Sadly, George was killed there, just two days before Christmas 1917 at Magdhaba. The allied troops were desperate to gain access to the wells at Magdhaba and the Light Horse, the Camel Corps, some New Zealand and British troops got out their bayonets for what has been called the last great cavalry charge to overcome a Turkish force greatly superior in number. George survived the charge through

4 Hector Holthouse *Gympie Gold* Angus & Robertson, Sydney 1973. P38

the Turkish trenches but when, mission accomplished, the horsemen pulled up to loosen their saddle-girths and to give their horses a rest, George fell from the saddle. One fatal shot from a sniper's bullet was all it took to take his life. He was the 2nd Light Horse's only casualty that day and they were the first of the victors to enter Magdhaba.

On his return to Gympie, my father wanted to join a Light Horse mate of his, Yorkie Booth, in a venture in New Guinea but his mother, understandably, wasn't happy with the idea and my mother, then on the scene, valued a secure job more highly than a risky venture in New Guinea. They went to Chillagoe. Even then, it was a troubled time. As Warden's clerk my father was instructed to destroy the records of certain private mining leases. With his mining heritage and belief in fair play, he couldn't do it. My mother found his reluctance hard to understand. 'It was only a little thing,' she complained, 'and after that he never got promotion for years.' It was the time of the 'Mungana Affair' and Dad was content. At least he could sleep conscience-free at night.

From Chillagoe they moved north to the Courthouse in Cooktown. It was 1925 and my sister, Jean, was born. She, like our father in early life (his hair darkened later) was a redhead, her downy hair of such a yellowy-gold colour that my mother's Aboriginal helper remarked that it looked 'alla same sucked mango'. Considering the old-time 'stringy' mangoes had myriads of fibres attached to the seed after the delicious pulp was consumed, it was a very apt description.

The family duly came to Nanango on my father's transfer from Cooktown. With his war service he was able to obtain some finance under a scheme available to returned soldiers to build a home there. Earlier, there had been a Soldiers Settlement Scheme to provide land for ex-soldiers to farm outside Cooktown. Dad was mildly interested but Mum wasn't at all impressed and probably rightly so, considering the distance from markets. The scheme was not successful. The house that was duly built was a lovely home, old 'Queenslander' style, black oiled weatherboards with a white painted trim high-lighting windows, doors, fascia and stairway. My parents were both keen gardeners and Mum had a colourful flower garden in the front while Dad grew his veges out the back. When Gran, our mother's mother and Zac's daughter, joined us, a yard for her cherished chooks was put up in the back yard. The house itself adjoined the town Common at the back. So did the maternity home run by Matron Macaboy. I was born there, almost next door, in late 1930.

The Great Depression

Like Queensland's earliest years, the thirties were a low point economically but this time the slump took in all Australia. It was the time of the Great Depression. Many 'travellers', mostly single men but sometimes whole families, going from place to place in search of work, camped on the Common, just over our back fence. There was also a spare allotment next door between us and a local shopkeeper's house. He used to stack disused wooden packing cases in the spare allotment. It was also fenced, so that travellers often put their horses in there and made quite a comfortable camp with wooden crate walls and a tent-fly roof. The wooden cases also served as useful tables, chairs and storage cupboards.

From as soon as I could toddle to the dividing fence, I spent as long as possible watching those lovely horses, hoping one day to have one of my very own. Usually my mother collected me and took me inside before I could make contact with any of the campers but, after a couple of years, I did get to the stage of discussing the purchase price of a little pony I'd fallen deeply in love with. Its owner humoured me and I had many lovely dreams until, one morning, I found broken-heartedly, that he and 'my' pony had moved on.

Most of the travellers didn't stay long. They were entitled to 'sustenance', a small payment for food, that they obtained at the Court House but they were encouraged to move on. Many took their enforced idleness hard and tried to work on whatever they could scavenge to make saleable items. In the days before washing machines and dryers, clothes were boiled-up in a 'copper', a big container made of that non-rust metal, rinsed several times with a final blue-bag rinse to enhance the whiteness, wrung out by hand (or, if you were lucky, with a hand-operated 'mangle') and pegged on a line to dry. The lines were long wires stretched from post to post or from obliging trees. This suited the swagmen. It made a market for hand-whittled wooden clothes pegs which usually outlasted their machine-made competitors and for forked clothes props. The forked props, trimmed from barked, very slender saplings, were used to raise the lines to optimum height. This could be conveniently low as the clothes were pegged out and raised to a maximum to be left to dry. The clothes pegs and props met a ready market at first but there was, unfortunately, a limit on the number of pegs and props needed.

Some clever men with rabbit traps offered rabbits – cleaned, dressed and ready to cook – for sale. The skins were carefully preserved and sold elsewhere. Some more dexterous artisans made lovely ornamental flower-pots from kerosene tins. The tins were rectangular on a base of a little over 30cms square and perhaps double that in height. The tops were cut out with tin snips, each side folded down and cut to a tapering triangular shape. This folded bit was then cut into vertical strips which were individually rolled up (using a wooden clothes peg) so that the overall effect was of metal curls cascading artistically down in an arrowhead arrangement. Gran bought some of these flower-pots, painted them a dark green and planted maiden hair and other ferns in them. They looked most effective. One old fellow stayed on the Common for a long period. He sought out odd-job work – chopping wood, mowing lawns with the old man-powered push mower of the time, tidying yards and gardening. He'd willingly try anything that gave him a little money to live on. Dad usually cut the wood for the stove in our house while my job was to collect the 'chips' to be used for early morning fire-lighting. Dad now relinquished his job to the old-timer who was also available for repairs and additions to Gran's hen roost and fowl yard. Gran was pleased with his work and, as well as paying the small sum asked, would take him a plate of that evening's meat and vegetables as he and Dad sat on the woodheap discussing the sorry state of the world.

It turned out, from what I overheard when Gran and Dad had been discussing him, that he had been a gem prospector working the Anakie field inland from Rockhampton. He had been successful at his calling but in hard times there was no money to buy useless things like gemstones, no matter how beautiful they were. Gran's husband had been an engineer at Monkland 7 and 8 goldmine at Gympie and she, like my father, took a keen interest in mining. The old fossicker brought out his sparkling stones to show us. They were polished and beautifully faceted to highlight their exquisite colours. My favourite was the biggest, a regal 'royal' – or castor oil bottle – blue. The others were a paler blue with some showing touches of green or pale gold tones. I knew, as soon as I saw them, that Anakie sapphires were the best in the whole world. I was entranced. Completely under their spell, I promised myself that, when I grew up I would go to Anakie and find my own jewels.

Eventually, the old fossicker moved on. Sometimes, the Police encouraged the swaggies to leave town but I don't know if the move was his decision or theirs. He was just not there any more but what I did know was that Dad became the owner of some of the lustrous sapphires, including the superb 'castor oil bottle' blue one. It later became, set in between some diamond chips, my engagement ring, a reminder of both men in my life, my Dad and my husband, Bill. Sadly, someone else liked it and, knowing that I took it off when I kneaded the bread dough and hung it on a special nail behind the kerosene fridge, helped himself. Years later I found that my prime (and only) suspect had earned himself an appropriate nick-name derived from his habits. He was called 'Hydraulic' because he'd 'lift anything'.

While the sad procession of travellers continued, the Depression spread to the locals with tragic results. One of my father's many titles at the Court House was the unhappy one of Coroner. My mother and Gran must have been away as I was spending the day in my Dad's care. We were going somewhere in a borrowed ute and I was eagerly waiting to take my place between Dad and the driver in the front seat. Two women on the street beside us were muttering and watching us with disapproving looks.

Tragedy at the Farm

"He's not taking the child!" one remarked in outraged disbelief to her friend.

I was furious and felt like telling her what I thought. I went everywhere with my Dad. They had no right….

Dad quickly interjected, "Get in," he ordered and I flew up to take my seat in the front of the ute, my feathers still considerably ruffled.

We drove first to a farmhouse where the usual cup of tea was brought out and I was soon left with the farmer's wife, a family friend, while her husband joined the others and drove off. When they returned, there was a layer of leafy boughs in the tray of the ute supporting a long, canvas-wrapped parcel with a nebulous swarm of noisy insects almost cloaking it. I was curious and moved to have a closer look only to be told by my father to "Keep back. Get in the car. They're bees."

I quickly did as I was told. I knew all about bees as I'd been stung on the finger while picking myself a bunch of Mum's champion Iceland poppies the day before the Flower Show. Mum said the bee sting would teach me a lesson. It did. I didn't have to be told a second time.

Many years later I heard the true story. The bees were, in fact, blowflies and the funny smell emanating from the canvas–wrapped bundle was from the decomposing body of a neighbouring farmer. Unable to find any way out of his deepening financial problems he decided to end his life. He sent his wife and children in to town to his in-laws on some pretext, for the weekend. He then proceeded to the outside lavatory, climbed onto the seat to attach a noose to the rafter, then, with his head engaged in the loop, jumped down from the seat. When his family returned from their outing he wasn't there. Worried, they went looking for him but his body wasn't found till the following morning – only one of several tragic suicides.

My Schooling Begins

Life went on and gradually things got better. The economy improved. Nanango shops even began to stock the new American chewing gum, a penny (1c) for a pack of four tangy tablets. My school life began at the beginning of the year I turned five. I knew a few words that my father had taught me and was really keen to learn to read and write. "Teach yourself to read, Possum," he advised me, " and you can teach yourself anything." Nowadays you can get videos to do that. Jean was five years ahead of me and though we used to walk to school together with our mates, braving at times the attacks of maniacal magpies, we each had our separate lives and circle of friends. During these hard times, a man toured our part of the State with a pair of camels. They were equipped with bench seats that would accommodate three or four children on each side of the hump. I was looking forward eagerly to my ride and was on my best behaviour to impress Mum. Jean wasn't interested. Despite my enthusiasm, like the rest of my co-riders, I felt more than a little shudder of trepidation when the huge animal rose awkwardly from its hooshed-down position prior to the start of the ride. It was a mind-boggling experience. Six decades later when the compilation *Voices from Elsewhere* was launched by my Morialta Writers' Group in Nanango, I wrote a short account of my early memories. It was published in the local paper and several readers wrote in recalling that same time in their lives. One man wrote to me mentioning the camel rides. He was very keen to go but was unable to score a ride. There were five kids in his family and at three pence (3c) a ride, his mother couldn't afford to waste that much money. Instead of feeling blessed, I felt more than a little bit mean that I was able to enjoy my ride while he had to miss out.

School began for me and my classmates in Prep 1, a Preparatory grade similar to what has been proposed to be re-introduced now. The Prep teacher was usually female, of mature years, and skilled not only in teaching children to read and write but also able to inspire them to want to succeed in these arts. We had copy books in which we inscribed page after page of 'pot hooks', curves a bit like fish hooks or letters 'J'. I think it was to teach us how to control our writing hand for the curves of cursive writing as we progressed further. For everyday use we had slates, readily cleaned with a sponge or a piece of rag brought to school for that purpose. We used slim little slate pencils to leave their mark on the slates.

We learnt the alphabet and how to spell and also learnt this by rote, repeating things over and over until they were committed to memory. These methods are not universally approved today but they seemed to work for us. To be able to recognise the sight and sound of the letters we repeated *(ad nauseum)* jingles to help us remember. 'a' like an apple on a stick. 'a' says 'a'. Capital 'A'was like an attic and said 'a' as in apple and attic. On the blackboard Teacher drew us a dear little curtained window at the top of 'A's' attic. 'c' was like a cake with a piece taken out and 'c' said 'ka' as in cake. 'T' was like a tree and said 'tuh'. By putting ka-a-tuh together you could hear the sound of 'cat'. Change the 'c' to 'm' (a 'much wider bridge) and you had 'mat', 'n' was a narrow bridge and Teacher drew trains crossing a wide 'm' and a narrower 'n' on the blackboard. An 'r' was like a rose in a vase and added to 'at' easily gave you 'rat'. From there it was only a short step to real reading – 'A cat sat on a mat.' Of course, 'a' didn't always say the same vowel sound and letters like 'ph' saying the same as 'f' complicated things a bit but, all in all, once we cracked the code we could solve most of the more simple sentences. This gave our egos quite a lift.

A generation later, I was the teacher and our son, John, my first pupil. The school was the Queensland Primary Correspondence School, a wonderful concept thought up in the 1930s for getting education out to where there were no schools. Lessons were mailed back and forth from outback pupils to their teacher/mentor in Brisbane. It was a great idea (which would have been better had we a regular mail service) but, to John, education meant learning to be a top horse- and cattle-man like his Dad. Paperwork – reading and writing – was only for girls. His Brisbane-based teacher, who had quickly become one of the family, suggested that John's younger sister Nancy, not yet five years old, might do the lessons (unofficially) with him. It worked out extremely well. John exerted himself to prove the superiority due to his greater age and the hours spent in school became almost enjoyable.

School practices were about to undergo a radical change. The old way of reading with the help of the letters was to be replaced by a newer and better method of 'Look and Say'. Dick and Dora (plus Nip and Fluff) took over from the cat on the mat and children were supposed to read simply by recognising the words. Again John's teacher made a wise suggestion. 'Keep John's old lesson papers for Nancy.'. We did and she quickly learnt to identify quite long words by their letter sounds. Years later this paid off when she was at University. Her lecturer was impressed and asked where she had done her first five years of school. Embarassed, Nancy owned up to Primary Correspondence with Mum and a year at the one-teacher school at Coen, halfway up the Peninsula where she was put up into John's grade as there were no other children for her class. 'I knew it!' he said, quite pleased with himself. 'You learnt the basics.'

As well as its early goldfield, Nanango had a commendable deposit of kaolin clay and, for a short time, produced excellent china and pottery. My mother had a beautiful china milk jug which, if tapped gently with a spoon or fork, rang clearly like a bell. Another prized possession was the Savanarola, a cabinet-sized machine that played the old, thick, black 78 records. My parents had a variety of records featuring Australian singers including Nellie Melba, plus Caruso and Dad's favourite at that time, the American negro Paul Robeson.

The Presbyterian Church which Gran and Mum attended regularly and to whose Sunday School Jean and I were dutifully sent each week, held a concert as well as their famous flower show each year as a fundraiser. At one concert, my mother, dressed to the nines as Nellie Melba, was centre stage besides the piano, miming Melba singing one of her popular ballads, *Coming Through the Rye*, while, behind the curtain someone was playing the record of the genuine Melba. Most of the crowd soon woke to the subterfuge and became rather vocal, alternatively boo-ing and cheering while my mother opened and shut her mouth in time to Melba's voice and tried to act like a famous diva. The crowd loved it and became even more rowdy until an elderly Scotsman could not bear it any longer. He stood up and shouted, 'Quiet! Give the lassie a chance! The young gel has a beautiful voice.' Luckily, the record was nearly finished as the performance fell a little flat after his remonstration.

Family Outings

When my father was discharged from the Light Horse, he saved to buy a Red Indian motorbike. With the acquisition of a wife, a side-car was added and this proved to be sufficient for both my mother and sister, but, when I arrived, the family had outgrown that means of transport. The motorcycle was put aside, but Dad stayed with his Native American predilections and purchased a Pontiac tourer car. Like the motorbike, it was a dark Indian red, one of those rectangular shaped vehicles with canvas hood and window shields of a perspex-like material that could be clipped on in case of rain or bleak weather. They were the windows. On each side, a running board greatly assisted the ladies as they climbed on board and also provided a travelling place for our collie dog, Lassie.

With the car, the whole family could go visiting. My mother, rather unusually for the times, learnt to drive also and often provided transport to the church ladies' socials and similar events. Some weekends, we took the car to visit friends on outlying properties. Manumbar was a favourite. At one place on Manumbar rosella bushes grew wild so that, when the fruit were mature, expeditions were made to collect them to make jam for family and friends and for sale at the Church fete. There were so many, they were picked by the kerosene tin bucketful and took ever so long to prepare before they could be boiled up to make the delicious jam. I'm sure that the women were relieved that the rosellas came only for a short time once each year.

At times Dad and I ventured out, on foot, on the bike or when he had to collect firewood, in the car by ourselves. My father didn't have a bad voice and we used to sing as we went along. One of his favourites was *Shenandoah*, and he told me the story of his great-uncle who had a ship called the *Shenandoah* and who was a pirate. This sounded very exciting. I knew all about pirates and could picture my great-great uncle James with his pirate outfit – skull and crossbones flag, wooden leg, patch over one eye and a talking parrot perched on his shoulder. Yo, ho, ho. It was a pleasing picture and gave me a lot of enjoyment. As I grew older, I began to realise that not every word fathers uttered should be taken as Gospel truth.

I was forgiving. It was a good story and tales of the dashing pirate's doings enlivened many a trip which might otherwise have been rather prosaic. Imagine my amazement, when, after Dad had died, I came across Cyril Pearl's book *Rebel Down Under* about the dashing Captain James Iredale Waddell who commanded the *Shenandoah* for the Confederate Navy in the American Civil War. He wasn't a pirate of course - or not in the eyes of the Southerners. He was a blockade runner.

The Damned Yankees had blockaded the eastern American seaboard to stop the Southerners from sending cotton to the idle mills in northern England.

At one time, the *Shenandoah* put in to Melbourne for repairs. Australia was neutral and it was permissible for ships from both sides to be assisted in times of need. But some eager stowaways joined the crew when it sailed out of Port Phillip Bay and taking on crew was a serious infringement of the laws of neutrality. The *Shenandoah* was finally apprehended and Captain Waddell was taken to court. Many Northerners wanted to make him walk the proverbial plank but he was a legal belligerent in a regular war. Besides that, he was such a Southern gentleman that few of his victims would give evidence against him. The confiscated *Shenandoah* was sold. The Sultan of Zanzibar bought her for a pleasure craft and re-named her the *Majidi* but she, with the rest of the Sultan's armada, was sunk in a hurricane in early 1879.

James Waddell, a very early Greenie, was in the Behring Strait attacking the Yankee whaling fleet when the South surrendered. He did not know and kept sinking. He can lay claim to firing the last shots of the American Civil War.

I loved going out to the farms with my father. At times he would ride out with our host to look at prime bullocks in the back paddock with me sitting proudly on a cushion in front of his saddle. At one place, a dairy farm, the inspection was done differently. The children brought the cows in for milking by riding an extremely docile milker's bullock instead of a pony. I was a little nervous to begin but I enjoyed the ride I was given once I quickly realised just how friendly the overgrown 'poddy' was.

The Ladies Guild

Both my mother and father played tennis and golf and were proficient enough to win the occasional trophy. Dad liked getting out bush, too, shooting a hare or a duck which Gran would stew up to make a delicious evening meal complete with dumplings floating on top. Gran and Mum's spare time was taken up mostly by the Presbyterian Ladies Guild, a fund-raiser for their church, and for other good causes. Gran was a fanatical crocheter. She made the daintiest of table centres using a needle so fine that its hook was barely visible. She also did tatting, making beautiful edgings around handkerchiefs which she suitably embroidered in one corner. Knitting was also one of her talents. She could never sit for long without some of her 'work' in her hands. Mum was a champion smocker and decked me out in exquisitely smocked frocks, the smocking gathering the full skirt to a little yoke. She also did 'romper suits' for boy babies. The blue-smocked tops were worn over baggy bloomer-like pants, roomy enough to conceal the mandatory terry-towelling nappy of those days before disposables. Her little dresses and romper suits were in great demand at the Church fetes. She was also a champion sponge cake maker. They all but floated off the serving plate when they were served up at parties. Dad preferred something more substantial like fruit or madeira cake for weekend smokos.

Mum was an enthusiastic bridge player and it was a rather competitive activity. Bridge groups met in player's homes in turn, with each hostess vying for perfection with an enjoyable bridge game followed by a mouth-watering afternoon tea in which the best china and silver was brought out for use. The 'best' sugar was in cube form and special silver tongs were used daintily to transfer sugar to cups. 'One lump or two?' With her crocheted tablecloths, Royal Doulton china, Sterling silver and her sponge cakes, my mother's hostess standing was rather high. Gran didn't usually play bridge, sitting on the verandah with her 'work' and coming in only to chat with her special friends once the game was over.

Occasionally something took us in to Nanango's big sister, the peanut capital of Kingaroy. To catch a train we went to Yarraman (an Aboriginal name for horse, I was told) some 20k south of Nanango as the rail line didn't come any further out.

Transfer to Goondiwindi

Public Servants such as Clerks of Petty Sessions didn't stay for long in one town. Transfers came every few years. My father was to move on to the Court House in Goondiwindi. It was a mixed blessing. New places are always exciting but the combined efforts of our parents and Gran had turned our Nanango home into such a beautiful place, its garden a show piece, that it was a wrench to leave it all behind. The Government arranged for the packing and the transport of furniture and personal goods but my mother didn't trust even the most professional of these packers with her beloved crystal and Royal Doulton. In those days, ladies' prizes at golf and tennis tended to be in the form of beautiful china or silverware and Mum also had a collection of fine china cups, saucers and plates, many given to her as 'going-away' gifts. Her 'crazy tea-set' or as she sometimes called it, her 'friendship tea-set,' was particularly well-loved. She used to save old 'milanese' and 'swami' petticoats, precursors of nylon underwear, with other soft materials, to use as wrapping for her treasures. They were carefully stowed in two large box-like travel cases kept especially for their transport. She insisted on packing these herself and the cases always travelled with her. I don't recall any breakages in transit.

The humdrum remainder of our belongings went to Goondiwindi by rail and were held in storage until a house could be found for us. We drove down in Ponty the Pontiac with Mum's precious cases taking pride of place. Sadly, our dog, Lassie, didn't accompany us. She died just before we were to leave.

Goondiwindi on the Border

Goondiwindi was a new experience to be enjoyed. It wasn't green farming country like Nanango but tended more towards wide golden expanses of grazing land. Wool, at the time, was king but there were also many properties given over to cattle and very prime beef cattle at that. Some grain was grown but it was foremost a pastoral area. Situated on the banks of the Macintyre River which ran into the longer Darling River, it was as far south as you could go without leaving the State of Queensland. The Macintyre River formed part of the New South Wales/Queensland border. In fact, in the centre of the bridge which spanned it was a metal plate about 30cms wide. We children loved to jump from side to side of it – there wasn't much traffic in those days – calling 'New South Wales' or 'Queensland,' depending on which side we'd landed. Because of its strategic position as regards N.S.W., the Goondiwindi rail line, extended from Brisbane in the first decade of the twentieth century, was in demand for the cartage of produce south. It was an important stop for interstate cattle which had to be checked carefully for the dreaded cattle-tick before they were allowed to cross the border.

Like Nanango, Goondiwindi took its name from a cattle station.[5]It was taken up by Sampson Marshall in 1838. He called it Gundawinda which was said to mean 'water running over rocks' in the native dialect. An alternative name and meaning is given as Goona Winna, a resting place of birds. Take your pick.

We were able to rent a very comfortable home, once the town house of an old grazing family, the Carringtons. It was another lovely Queenslander and was set on an enormous allotment, four times the size of a normal house block and spanning the distance between two streets. A long row of delightfully shady pepperina trees lined one fence, a wonderful place for a succession of cubby houses. The garage, which backed onto the street at the rear, had been old stables and a carriage house. When Dad pointed this out to me I began to visualise an ideal stable for my dream pony- when I could talk my mother into letting

5 *New National Australian Encyclopedia* Horwitz, Sydney. 1974 p377

me have one. The shrubs in the garden suited the drier climate and there was even a bearing fig tree, the first real live one I had ever seen, beside the house. The figs were delicious, far too nice to be made into jam. Gran and Mum were both compulsive jam-makers, especially if the Church had some fund-raising planned.

Parade Time

My mother continued with her round of bridge and tea parties with the crazy tea-set arriving quite unharmed. We came to Goondiwindi at about the same time as two rather miraculous events. Goondiwindi had its town power upgraded, with the main thoroughfare sporting bright lights carried on tall concrete columns, most impressive. A procession was organised with just about everyone taking part. Jean's class at school were learning eurythmics and, dressed in multi-coloured classic dresses and somewhat reminiscent of Greek nymphs and maidens, they marched and performed for the occasion. The second headliner was the news that a Canadian couple, the Dionnes, had just produced quintuplets by natural conception. They all survived. That, too, was an event to be celebrated. One of Mum's old bridge group ladies from Nanango was also in Goondiwindi. Her husband, a bank manager, was transferred just before we made the move and her son, Donald, had been one of my playmates. Once the mothers got their heads together, it was quickly decided that Donald and I would join the parade highlighting the world's first surviving quins. Donald was outfitted in a suit and bowler hat, with a stethoscope draped over one shoulder to show that he represented the world-famous Dr. Defoe. I was more simply dressed as the anonymous nurse in a plain white dress with a veil to match. The pram I pushed was no problem but gathering up five identical celluloid baby dolls (of real baby size) was a more difficult task. I had a baby doll, as did Jean. Donald, of course, didn't have one and the three remaining quins were hard to come by. They had to be 'identical'. But we found them and once they were assembled, the mothers set to work creating suitable baby clothes, very fancy and all with the same motif. Once completed, the pramful created quite a lot of interest as they took their place in the parade.

One of my daily duties was to collect milk from a woman who lived a short distance away at the end of the street. It was before the time of bottled or carton milk and though there was probably a milkman who delivered fresh milk to the back door, Mum preferred to give her custom to Mrs. Christmas. She had two milking cows, a big black and white Friesian and a red cow, not as tall, but very solid. The red cow was called Bessie. Mrs. Christmas was fine-boned and tiny. She was smaller than my sister Jean. Her charges dwarfed her so much that I was extremely puzzled one morning when I went down to get the milk. Mrs. Christmas only half-filled the small enamel billycan. 'Tell your mother that's all

I can spare. Bessie up and died on me.' I put the lid carefully on the billy and hurried home to tell Mum the startling news. Mrs. Christmas looked all right to me, but Bessie was such a huge animal by comparison, that I couldn't work out how Mrs. C. had managed to escape from underneath when Bessie died 'on' her. Mum didn't seem inordinately concerned when I passed on the information but merely expressed the hope that Mrs.Christmas would replace Bessie as soon as possible.

Gran soon obtained some chooks to keep her occupied and us supplied with eggs. She needed something to do in those very early hours when she wasn't knitting, crocheting or engaged in household chores. Dad often threw a fishing line in, or left a set-line along the river bank and, checking daily, kept us fairly well supplied with fish, mostly the legendary yellowbelly for which the Macintyre was duly famous. He often fished two lines at a time. The 'set' line had a 'bell' made from a small, round, deep-sided tobacco tin with a steel nut-on-wire clapper. The bell was supposed to ring when a fish nibbled at the bait. Most times it worked well, alerting the fisherman. Dad also shot or trapped rabbits along the river flats. Rabbit stew featured often on the menu of both our home and on our friends' tables. Dad collected the skins and gave them to another friend who was a rabbit trapper, but I collected the fluffy, white tails when the rabbits were skinned. I had some idea of bordering a red velvet cape with them – something like the King's ermine-trimmed Coronation robes.

Following Dad along the river bank led me to try to make my first pact with God. To my mother's disgust I still preferred going barefoot to wearing the shoes she bought me. Dad didn't seem to mind and told me that, in the old Scottish Highlands, despite the cold, women often went barefoot, by choice and not by necessity. Mum definitely did not favour this idea. On this occasion I found myself, barefoot, and stranded in the thickest patch of bindi-eyes (khaki burr) I've ever experienced. Dad was too far ahead to come to my assistance as I struggled to escape, getting more prickles in my fingers as well as in my feet as I battled to be rid of them. My Sunday School upbringing offered a chance of salvation. 'Get me out of this, please God, and I'll never go barefoot again.' I managed to struggle out alive and did, for a while, wear shoes, but I'm afraid, like most humans, I did not completely honour my promise.

With most of the town's population, the whole family assembled on the riverbank one afternoon to watch what was thought to be a record flood in the Macintyre River. The water was very high, a milk-chocolate colour and the current was very strong and swift. A few drowned sheep and a bloated cow floated down in a motley mix of debris. While I felt sorry for the animals, I think what upset me and my friends most of all was the bobbing horde of watermelons that sped past, well out of reach. A Chinaman's garden on the riverbank upstream traditionally provided the mouth-watering melons for our school break-up and Christmas parties. What would we do now? It was too awful to bear thinking about.

Playing Jacks

Some weekends we visited friends at Callandoon or Llandenny. I loved these outings. On the best occasions I was led around on a quiet and compliant horse for a short ride. Llandenny, which was the home of old friends of Gran's, had mostly sheep and Gran collected enough sheep knuckle-bones to make me a set of 'jacks'. When we returned home, she cleaned them thoroughly and dyed the jack bones a distinctive purple with indelible pencil and I soon became reasonably proficient in playing jacks. To do this, four knuckle-bones were placed in the corners of a small square, the fifth jack being held in the hand. The idea was to throw the hand-held jack in the air and, before it hit ground, to pick up one of the corner jacks and to catch the air-borne one. This move was continued until all four jacks were safely picked up. If one was dropped, your 'turn' ended. A repeat performance produced a similar action but this time, while the thrown jack was in the air, the corner jacks had to be carefully replaced. It was a game that was quite popular and I suppose it helped to make us more dexterous. Gran said that she used to play jacks when she was little and made me a pretty little cloth dilly-bag to carry and to store the jacks in.

The few years we spent in Goondiwindi soon passed. It was a pleasant time, lots of schoolmates, plenty of things to do and, best of all, those weekend trips to Llandenny and Callandoon. Dad received word of another transfer and soon Mum was again packing her precious tea-set with new keepsake cups, saucers and plates given as farewell gifts by her Guild and bridge friends. This time our destination was Tully – the wettest place in Australia – and so far away to the North that we must all go by train and leave poor old Ponti the Pontiac car behind. After farewelling friends, we boarded the rattly little train for Brisbane. From there we would travel almost the whole length of the Queensland coast (or so it seemed to me after Dad pointed Tully out on a map) to our new home.

The Wettest Town

The trip up the coast to Tully was a real adventure. I don't remember if the train had then been given the name of the Sunlander but the land we travelled through was beautiful, bright and sunny. We had a 'sleeper' and by day, Dad and I sat by the windows on the long bench seats while Mum and Jean read or 'rested'. Looking out the windows had a small downside. If you became too carried away with the scene before you and put your head outside the window, you were apt to get eyefuls of soot from the chugging steam engine. That was easily remedied and with Dad telling me where we were and what people did for a living in the districts we passed through, I was getting a very good geography lesson without knowing it.

First Sighting of Zebu Cattle

One sight I won't forget was just north of Rockhampton, on the open plains of Waverly where a small herd of most extraordinary animals grouped to watch us go past. They looked more like cattle than horses or even donkeys – definitely not camels, though they did have humps. Not the usual red, red and white or even black, they were a dirty grey and had huge lumps on top of their shoulders, very elongated, droopy ears that hung almost to their knees and the most gigantic up-curving horns. I'd never seen anything like them, even in a book.

'They're Zebus,' Dad explained. 'They use them to pull ploughs in India.'

These didn't come from the sub-continent, or at least, not directly. They were imported from the United States in 1933 by the Government (C.S.I.R.O., the research organisation that did so much useful work for farmers, cattlemen and others in Australia) and a syndicate of venturesome cattlemen who thought that an infusion of this tropical strain would improve the performance of cattle in the North. Apart from being able to handle the tropical heat with ease, they were also resistant to the ticks that decimated the northern cattle herds after their illicit entry through the Northern Territory in the 1890s. Those who put their faith in the Zebu bloodlines were proved right but I didn't have the slightest idea then that, some thirty years later, my husband and I would become early members of the society formed to accelerate their acceptance. This was the Australian Zebu Breeders Society later to become, with the later import of graded-up cattle from the United States, the more Americanised Australian Brahman Breeders Association.

Jean, a confirmed bookworm, read for most of the journey, oblivious to interesting things like hump-backed cattle and Mum, when not 'resting' got out her crochet though she often complained about how it quickly got dirty from the infiltrating soot. Dad and I were the only real sight-seers. The train made convenient stops along the way at Railway Refreshment Rooms where meals and delicious snacks were available and there was also a 'dining car' which provided the same facilities. It was like a never-ending picnic. At night, a railway employee came to each sleeping compartment and, pressing the right buttons and pulling the correct levers, converted the bench seat and its padded back-rest into fairly comfortable (though narrow) double-decker beds made up with pillows, sheets and a blanket. I much preferred the more exciting top bunk although it was a little too high to allow me to gaze out the window at the country we passed.

Our arrival at the Tully platform was a little disappointing. The town was then keeping its distance from the railway and we had to drive some distance in a taxi before we saw houses and shops. We pulled up at our destination, a hotel in the main street, 'Pat and Mick's', owned by the Mullins brothers, that was to be our temporary home.

Early Days of Sugarcane

While the Tully that we found was only a relatively young town, it had its origins way back in the nineteenth century. The gallant Kennedy made his courageous journey through much of the district after he was landed at Rockingham Bay on his fateful trip to Cape York. That was in 1848. Just seventeen years later, a Scotsman, John Ewen Davidson, with his partner E.D.Thomas[6], came from Oxford University and a later stint in the cane plantations of the West Indies, to take up land on the Murray River. We know it today as Bellenden Plains. He was hoping to establish a sugar industry on the rich coastal plains and even brought materials with him to erect a small crushing mill. Though no fault of Davidson's, it wasn't a very auspicious undertaking.

The indigenous people resented the intrusion and his partner and most of the employees left, citing the threat of native attack. By the end of 1866, a cyclonic flood, 'swept away most of the cane and inundated the intended mill site'. [7] Some 'broken bricks' and a few 'pits' were all that were left to tell the story.

6 *Tully Sugar Mill Golden Jubilee Book 1925-1975*

7 *Tully Mill Golden Jubilee Book 1925-1975*

James Tyson, who among other noteworthy things gave his name to the majestic mountain that overlooks the town, tried growing cane again in 1881 using Kanaka labour. Brice Henry, another well-known name in Tully's story, wrote that his parents came to the small cane-growing community with the 'Tyson pioneers'. The lack of a mill didn't deter them. They made their own sugar by 'smashing the joints of the cane with a hammer' and crushing it through a gigantic, hand-operated mangle. 'Burnt coral' was the 'lime' used in the refining process and their resulting sugar was better than the 'second-grade dark sugar' then available.

Soldier settlement was tried after World War 1 leaving in the area the Middle Eastern names of El Arish and Feluga. Sugar mills were built along the coast. South Johnstone opened its mill in 1915 and crushed its first cane the following year. Tully, at the time hampered by lack of ready access, missed out. E.G. (Big Ted) Theodore was a Minister in the post-war Labor Government who had great faith in the future of the North. When he became Premier in 1919, the settlers of Banyan and Tully worked with renewed optimism. On a visit to the area he assured them that the coastal railway would be completed and Tully linked with Cairns. With that access, a sugar mill would follow. A *Sugar Works Act of 1922* led to the construction of the mill with lighting, roads and bridges, at a cost of 765,000 pounds ($1,530,000) in 1925. When we arrived, thirteen years later, Tully had all the marks of a prosperous little town.

Tully for some reason, had a very large Finn population. Italians and Greeks, coming from the warmer Mediterranean, were to be expected on the sugarcane farms but to find so many Finns was surprising to us. My best mate at school, Sanni, had a Finn background as did our mutual friend Toini whose son Greg Norman later gained worldwide fame in the game of golf. A Finn carpenter, John, was building a home for rental on the slopes of Mt. Tyson, Brannigan Street, the last street up the hill and near the town's water reservoir. Dad had already been shown the house, another Queenslander, and took Mum up to view it. It gained her whole-hearted approval. We could take up residence as soon as it was completed, in about a month.

A House is Built

As usual (Jean seemed to cause very few upsets) I upset the plans by catching German measles, a childhood disease rather prevalent at the time. We left the hotel and took up temporary residence in a nearby house that was fortunately available for short-term rent. My spots and fever had long gone when we moved up the hill to our new home. John and his men took great pride in their work and used the beautiful local timbers, the cedar, silky oak and black bean to produce a stunning effect. Even the internal walls were of quarter-cut silky oak with that lovely ribbon of silk running through them. Built on a slight slope, the base was excavated to put the house on an even keel. The kitchen was reached from the backyard by a short flight of steps from a landing. A second flight led from the landing down to the laundry, a shower room and a rather large room known as 'John's room'. He stored some of his gear there a while and Dad promised it would always be there should John need storage or accommodation. He used it a few times but soon shifted his gear and moved on. The room became my private retreat.

'Laundry' is a bit of an overstatement for the place where Mum did the family wash but even it was 'state of the art' for the times. There was an impressive brick fireplace which featured a built-in copper . There was also a row of three up-to-date concrete tubs set at bench height along the wall. The brick copper-stand was a welcome improvement to the old cast-iron ones which were usually out in the weather and most homes still used the old-fashioned set of three circular galvanised tubs. Modernity continued upstairs with built-in kitchen cupboards, a linen cupboard sharing the bathroom wall and, separating the bedrooms, double walls which secreted space for built-in wardrobes. None of my schoolmates had 'built-in 'robes' at the time and, until they learned the secret, could never find the ones who were in the know when we played hide-and-seek. Though once or twice our giggles gave us away, especially when we heard their steps as they went to the window probably guessing that we'd jumped out.

Like the Nanango house, the exterior weatherboards were oiled black, window frames and fascia painted white. The big dining room/lounge with the beautiful arched divider, complete with pedestal stand either side for Mum's brass jardinieres, opened either through a 'cloak room' where hat, umbrellas and raincoats were stored, or through double French doors onto a corner verandah with the most outstanding view of the town and its valley. A second, longer stairway led to the front yard from the verandah.

Gran joined us once we'd settled in and, following the precedent set by other Brannigan Street residents with hens, John the builder had annexed part of the land outside the back fence for a chook run and built a neat little fowlhouse, all netted in against predatory carpetsnakes who lived on the mountain and with roosts and laying boxes. Gran was impressed and soon arranged for the poultry to move in.

The legitimate backyard also housed a large double garage and the 'little house', the outside toilet, whose 'dunny can' was removed and replaced in the middle of the night at regular intervals by a mysterious man called the 'nightman'. I believe he doubled in daylight hours as the 'rubbish man'. Unlike the hen house, the 'little house' wasn't snake-proofed which made night-time visits rather scary.

Mum and Gran soon made the area under the house an attractive place. Ferns and coloured-leaved plants grew along the bank of the excavation to a bed along the house's perimeter. Hanging baskets of ferns were suspended from the outer bearers. The area under the front steps also sported a lush garden of ferns with a stepped-up rockery surmounted by a luxuriant crows nest fern. Gran kept the gardens watered and in summer often hosed the dirt 'floor' making the place into a delightful refuge from the tropical summer heat..

Gran had left us to return to Gympie for a holiday. Her only son, Wallace, had suffered severe head injuries in an accident and the family were considering leaving the farm. Gran went down by train to see if she could help. She returned, in due course, with a present for me. My Aunt Claire, from whom I'd received my second Christian name, had been a gifted violinist before her death from a meningitis-type fever before she reached the age of twenty-one. As she had survived being thrown from an overturned sulky by a bolting horse on her return from a concert, her death seemed unfair. Both she and her main concern, her violin, were unhurt in the accident but her good luck didn't persist.

Music Lessons

Great-grandfather Zac Skyring had made a violin, of native timber, with a 'full' back rather than the two matched halves of the orthodox instruments. Gran would have liked this one but it couldn't be found, so she came home with Claire's fiddle for me. Zac had also made a piano of choice local cabinet timbers but Gran didn't waste time trying to locate it. Carrying it on the train would have been more than she could manage. Many decades later, I heard that the piano had indeed been found, reconditioned and put on display in the Gympie Mining Museum. I'd love to see it. With Aunt Claire's violin came a gift from Gran of violin lessons. I was eight years old, going on for nine. Mrs. Morton, the Tully Methodist minister's wife would teach me. Gran, Dad and I were early risers, up with the sun, but Mum liked to sleep in to a more civilised hour. My practising, especially the initial rather discordant, tread-on-the-cat's-tail noises, weren't appreciated. Dad could flee to his vege garden, Gran to her chooks, but Mum was stuck with me, in the house with just a double wall between us. Mrs. Morton solved the problem. I could leave my violin with her at the church and practise in the room where we went for Sunday School. That suited me fine, but it meant going to school a different way. The shortcut with Joan was 'out'. Instead, I went the long way with Micky and Jill Byrnes who lived behind the church, accompanied of course by Winkie who waited patiently while I practised. He didn't howl, either.

Scales and studies were apt to get a bit boring after a while, but, in the Sunday School room was a large cupboard filled with hymnals and other music. I had a ball trying them out.

Mrs. Morton was rather impressed by my violin and used to borrow it to play at concerts later put on by the Red Cross and the Comforts Fund. Not only did it have a lovely tone, it was also very old. A yellowed piece of paper inside it told that it was a Stainer, made in Absam (wherever that was) in the year that Captain Cook and his *Endeavour* sailed along our eastern coast, 1770. Its tone also impressed the music examiner, Sydney May, who came yearly to conduct the examinations. I think its superiority might have helped me to get me such high marks. After talking to my father and Mrs. Morton, Mr. May took the violin back to Sydney with him. He would take it to some experts there, Smiths. Gran was pleased that someone else readily saw the value in the family violin. Mrs. Morton let me use a more modern instrument of hers and, only a few weeks later, Mr. May who had to return to Townsville, drove up from there to share the good news with us. It was a genuine Stainer, in good condition and valued at 300 guineas. A guinea was a pound ($2) plus a shilling (10c) but at that time Dad's annual salary was almost the equivalent of the violin's valuation. We didn't want to sell it. The monetary value didn't impress me so much as the fact that a famous man like Sydney May liked it so much that he went to the trouble to take it to Sydney for a second opinion.

The Tully State Primary School was an object of pride. It was a large two-story brick building with play areas and store-rooms underneath and class rooms at the head of the impressive outside steps. A wide verandah ran along the length of the building with the Headmaster's Office and the Teachers' Common Room situated at the top of the steps in the mid-section of the building. Two less impressive wooden buildings, the Domestic Science and the Manual Training buildings, lay behind the main school. Next door was the Catholic School with its lovely statue of Our Saviour raising his hands in blessing – on the State School. My convent friends said we were in most need of them.

For Jean, her year at the Tully school was also her last year. She was in Scholarship class or Grade 7. A student had to pass 'Scholarship', a statewide examination, to be enrolled in a secondary or high school. The highlight of the Scholarship exam was the Lilley Medal, awarded to the student who gained the highest marks in the State. You can imagine our unbounded pride when one of our Grade Sevens, Enid Andrews, was the Lilley Medallist of her year. We all took some share in her glory. Her brother Bevan was in my class with he and I taking turns at coming top. On one occasion we even tied for the honour and Bevan, not usually so gallant (he used to amuse himself by jamming the end of my pig-tail in the little inkwell on the desk) allowed me to take the place of honour, first on the left, back row in the class room. Bevan didn't quite come up with the Lilley Medal but made it to the first twenty, students who were eagerly sought after by the secondary schools. Considering the size and the comparative isolation of the Tully school, we did very well.

Cruising on the *Sapphire*

After Scholarship, Jean went on to Blackheath Presbyterian Girls College in Charters Towers and life went on much the same for the rest of us. Dad was a keen fisherman at heart and we often spent the weekend at the mouth of the Hull River where the fishing was good and where a friend, Benny Barnett, often called with his boat the *Sapphire.* Benny sometimes took Dad and me on his mail run to the islands in the Family Group. Hugo Brassey was on Dunk Island and the Cohen sisters and later, Noel Woods on Alison or Bedarra Island. On the way we wove through many enticing islets and I got caught nicely when Benny pulled in at Goold Island to show something to Dad. The water was so crystal clear that the seabed was very much in view. Thinking it was only about knee-deep, I jumped off the boat. A split second later my hat floated off and was rescued by Benny while Dad rescued me when I re-surfaced.

Hugo Brassey was a very entertaining man or else I was a very good audience. He told me one story that I had trouble believing. His mother, who was wife to a Governor General, died at sea on their return to England. Hugo told me that they threw her body overboard. I found this a bit hard to believe even though it was Hugo who told the story. I was rather ashamed and apologetic many years later when I came by a beautiful quarter-calf bound book, *The Last Voyage* by Lady Brassey. A folding map showed 'the track of the Yacht *Sunbeam*, November 1886 to December 1887' and, at a point in the Indian Ocean, roughly midway between Western Australia's North West Cape and Java (Indonesia), was a small cross. It marked the spot where Lady Brassey, with due ceremony, had been buried at sea. Hugo also told me that I could have the little island, Purtaboi, that nestled happily in Brammo Bay. I totally believed in this generous gift and made many plans to live there 'when I grew up.' I would be a beachcomber.

At times, Dad helped Benny with his cargo. One occasion was when the Cohen sisters decided to build their dream home on Bedarra. It was in a cove, roughly a back-to-front E shape with the long side facing out to sea. One 'leg' of the E was the open-plan living/dining room, the middle was bedrooms and the last wing was their artists' studio. They were both very talented. The building was made of pise, an old medium but very trendy in those days. The sisters' artistic vision didn't end there. The place was lined and ceiled with bamboo. It was really something extraordinarily beautiful to see. The bamboo was split laterally and applied to the surfaces in geometric designs. One room had a ceiling with diamond shaped motifs surrounded by an intricate patchwork of the curved bamboo. It was most effective and unusual. Even the large sideboard had the vertical back to its top decorated with a design in small bamboo.

Getting the bamboo was when Benny and the *Sapphire* came in – and Dad and me. On the mainland at Clump Point was a grove of the tall bamboo. It was just about all that was left when a cyclone destroyed the Mission at the adjoining Mission Beach early in the twentieth century. Lengths of the bamboo were cut, tied into bundles and loaded onto the *Sapphire* to be transported to the building site. As the bamboo was relatively light, I was allowed to help and at least, I could carry the saw and the tomahawk for the working party of porters.

Incidentally, it was at Mission Beach that I met up with my first electric fence, an ultra-modern contrivance I had never even heard of. Touching a wire to get through to watch some cows and calves feeding along the creek bank I was immediately knocked flat. Dad rescued me, unhurt, and pointed out, with a straight face, that had I not been barefoot but wearing the new sandshoes Mum had bought me, the rubber soles would have earthed the current and negated the effect of the electricity. It didn't help either to hear him and Benny sniggering over my misfortune when they thought I was out of earshot.

We visited Dunk Island as a family a couple of times, staying in the little 'chalets' under the coconut palms and having meals at the 'big house'. Hugo told me about E.J. 'Ted' Banfield, the man who made Dunk his home. Banfield's father had been in the newspaper business in Victoria. Ted followed in his footsteps as a reporter, later doing editorial work for the early Townsville papers. With his health failing rapidly, his doctor advised him to retire. He took his doctor's advice and with his wife, Bertha, Banfield spent twenty-five fruitful years on the island writing several books about his experiences. A cairn marked his gravesite on Dunk and an inscription paid tribute to 'The Beachcomber's' many-faceted nature.

'If a man does not keep pace with his companions
Perhaps it is because he hears a different drummer.
Let him step to the music which he hears.'

I thought the inscription was very apt and, finding some domestic rules and regulations rather tedious, decided to step to the music that I heard.

When we made our trips to the mouth of the Hull, we usually camped in a little one-roomed humpy whose walls were made of kerosene tins that had been opened-up, tops and bottoms removed and the sides flattened to make a sheet of useful building material. The roof was part kero tin, part re-cycled galvanised iron. A small lean-to with a chimney housed the open fire over which Mum and Gran cooked. The menu was mainly fish, thanks to Dad and his mates.

One Christmas, Jean had a friend, Lily, staying with her and Dad erected a small marquee tent beside the shack for Gran and us girls. One night there was a terrible storm. The rain bucketed down and water quickly lodged in the tent's sagging canvas roof. Gran decided to fix it. Grabbing her trusty black umbrella, she prodded the drooping canvas, hoping to dislodge the water that threatened to flatten our tent. Something went wrong. The rather sharp umbrella tip, plus the heavy weight of the water, caused the canvas to split. The tent was soon almost in two pieces and we struggled to escape from underneath it to the hut with our bedding and belongings. Next day was fine, so no great harm was done (except to the poor tent). It was certainly something to talk about when school started up again.

Lily and her brothers were of Russian descent and their surname was 'Roman'. They were a mysterious family said to have come from an exotic-sounding place, Vladivostok and were really 'Romanoff', descendants of the Russian Royal Family assassinated by the Bolsheviks during the Russian Revolution. We were all most impressed with the possibility, though Lily and her brothers were rather reticent. However, their close friends were the Vitte family and we had heard that was the surname of a trusty supporter of the Tsar and Tsarina.

Jean, Lily and the boys spent most of their time on the sea-front, beach-combing and swimming while I took my fishing rod, a slender, springy branchlet and went fishing in the river near a deep hole containing the murky snag of a large dead tree. It was supposed to be a good spot for fish but if I didn't get any bites after a short period of trying, I often dived in and tried to walk along the submerged trunk. This usually caused a local identity who sat a little further down with his hand-line to mutter disapprovingly, 'Groper bait!' A giant fish with a huge mouth, a groper, was said (by him) to live by the submerged snag. I survived and, after all these years, still haven't seen a real, live groper.

At times I went along the beach collecting small shells for my mother's oldest sister, Aunt Jean. Aunt Jean was a very remarkable woman living her life fully to within a few weeks of her hundredth birthday. As a young woman she went to central Queensland to the Atherton family as a lady's companion/governess and ended up by marrying not one, but two of the Atherton sons. Her first husband was killed early in their marriage leaving her with a small family to care for. She later married her husband's brother and had a second family but again, their happiness didn't last. He, too, died young. The wedding photograph taken of her first wedding, with my mother, then five or six years old, as flowergirl was rather interesting. As her second husband was best man for that wedding it shows her in wedding regalia in the company of both her husbands. I had heard of 'shotgun weddings' – this one was definitely not one – but my mother pointed out in the sepia-coloured studio photo a stockwhip in the lap of the little pageboy kneeling at the seated bridegroom's feet. The lad, Henry Daniels, had been rather unwilling to get dressed up to play the role of flowergirl's escort. He was won over when he was told that if he acceded Jean would give him a present. 'Would she give me a stockwhip?' She would and it was impossible to separate him from his cherished gift during the photography session. Her gift and his proud pleasure is there for all to see.

Fortunately, there was a big family of Athertons including James who went furrther north pioneering and had the far northern town named for him. When Jean was widowed a second time, a spinster sister of the grooms made her home with Jean and helped her greatly over the years. Jean was a wonderful worker and couldn't bear to be idle. She was an excellent seamstress and worked in conjunction with the David Jones store doing alterations and making dresses and underwear. Like Gran, she was also a crochet addict and made dozens of beautiful rugs. Her interests weren't limited to those habitually considered feminine. At one stage she grew mushrooms in a dis-used railway tunnel and did quite well. As she was of an artistic bent and as trinkets like necklaces, bracelets and ear-rings were hard to find during the war, she also took up jewellery making . As well as the little shells, I would collect for her the tiny pine-conelike seeds of the she-oak and any little gumnuts or gidi-gidi beans I thought would be suitable for 'beads'. She had no drill to bore the necessary hole for the thread but patiently burnt through the 'bead' with a red-hot darning needle. The resulting accessories were very decorative and she found a ready market for them. When Mum went to Sydney I always made sure she took a bag of shells and seeds for Aunt Jean.

Mountaineering

We didn't spend all our spare time at the coast. There were quite a few children in our street and I had a lot of mates. Micky (Margaret) and Jill Byrne lived at one end and Joan Mangan and her brothers Pat and Billy were just opposite us at the other end. Joan went to the Convent school so we could often walk to school together taking the short cut. Joan's brothers and their mates used to go on expeditions into the 'scrub' on Mt. Tyson. They were rather reluctant to add girls to their party but gave in sufficiently to let us accompany them to the Bottom Spring. It was high adventure. The biggest danger was stinging tree, but we knew where to find the antidote, the tuberous root of a little shiny-leafed evergreen plant that conveniently grew nearby. If applied immediately, it was quite efficacious. Possibly our worst problem was leeches. They seemed to be able to creep up and hide on our limbs and bodies without being noticed until they began their meal. Salt sprinkled on their engorged bodies soon got them to shrivel up and release the hold on their food source but they left a nasty itch.

We took sandwiches with us but loved also to take small potatoes which we baked in the coals of our tea-billy fire. If at all possible we took a tin of condensed milk as well, an expensive but well-cherished luxury. Making fires in what is today 'rainforest' sounds appalling but we never caused any problems. No fire ever got away and we left our dinner-camp site look almost identical to the way we found it.

After a few trips without any disasters, the boys allowed us to tag along to the Middle Spring. Top Spring, at a small waterfall near the mountain's summit, was definitely out of bounds to us. In fact, the boys hadn't yet been successful in reaching that high point themselves.

Enter the Winkie Family

My father's activities were much more interesting than my mother's. Gran had her chooks and could tell intriguing tales about when she was growing up outside Gympie. She was a young girl when her family made the arduous wagon trip from Brisbane to the goldfield and could tell of some very unusual happenings. Any spare time left from her knitting and crocheting was spent visiting friends, often younger than she was, who were housebound. Mum's concerns were the housekeeping (not a speck of dust to be seen), her garden, the Ladies Guild and her bridge parties. I much preferred Dad's diversions especially when they involved going out in the car Dad bought, to Winkelmuller's after scrub turkeys. Rudi Winkelmuller was an interesting man. He worked in the engineering section of the sugar-mill as a sort of boilermaker/fitter and turner and could make or fix anything. Being a turkey shooter, he had a special skill with rifles. The two Police, Tapsell and Kimlin, also Dad's mates and keen fishermen and turkey-hunters, put Dad in touch with Rudi. He could 'blue' rifles that were starting to go rusty in the humid climate and would soon have any defective sights readjusted and taking perfect aim. The Winkie's lived on a small acreage along the Jarrah Creek Road.

There were six kids in the family, going from Charlie who was four and a half weeks older than me, through Theresa, Helen, Anne, Irene to the baby, 'Bub' or, more formally, Katherine. Their mother, Irene, was Greek and a very talented woman. Dad often went turkey shooting with Rudi while I stayed to play with Charlie and Theresa. Rudi used turkey dogs trained not only to track the turkeys but also to 'point' when the startled bird flew up into a tree. If the shooter couldn't find the bird at Pluto's first 'point', the dog would go over to the man and point anew from that position, a ploy that rarely failed and we were regularly treated to turkey fricassee or delicious stew.

With his gun now re-conditioned, a set of wheels and a turkey-shooting mate, Dad (and Rudi) decided that Dad needed a dog of his own. Rudi had just the one, a half-grown black and tan pup. We called him Rudi. He kept this name for a few days until, on the kitchen landing, he was admonished for advancing a tentative puppy paw over the line separating the human kitchen from the less discriminatory landing. He quickly fled down the stairs but not before leaving, to Mum's disgust, a tell-tale puppy puddle on the landing. Dad decided on a name-change from the discredited Rudi. Gran suggested 'Winkie',

Irene's soubriquet, and from then on we held both Winkie Lady and Winkie Dog in high regard.

Winkie Dog promptly learned to sleep in his own quarters in a half-tank behind the garage and near the woodheap but, until he was fed and tied up for the night, he never let Dad or me out of his sight. He'd escort me to school whether by the shortcut over the spring or the long way round, taking in a stop for music practice. Having seen me safely to the school gate (no dogs allowed inside) he'd return to the Court House. There he'd stay, minding Dad and his off-sider Miss Roberts until school came out. Without fail, he'd be waiting at the school gate at 3.30. We couldn't work out how he was able to tell the time so accurately. Surely, he wouldn't have heard the school bell from the Court House more than a block away.

War is Declared

Our happy, carefree lives were soon shattered by an announcement from Prime Minister Robert Menzies. Germany had invaded Poland and on 3rd September, 1939, Britain declared war on Germany. Her action was immediately followed by France but within 45 minutes of Britain's announcement, Menzies declared war on behalf of Australia. We may have been third in line for the actual declaration but the 'honour'[8] of the 'first Allied shot of World War 2' went to a R.A.N. base at Port Nepean which fired its guns to prevent a German ship from leaving Port Phillip Bay in Victoria.

The war soon absorbed most of our thoughts. I even scored a whack across the rump with Dad's big, black umbrella for making a noise when he had his ear glued to the big, bulky and not very efficient, radio trying to catch the latest news of the war. I think it was the only 'corporal punishment' he even dealt out to me and it came as a distressing shock. He wanted to enlist, but was told that, at over forty years of age, he was too old. In any case, young men were more than willing to volunteer for service in the three armed forces. One of Jean's and my cousins joined the Airforce and was soon flying Lancaster bombers over Europe, another was a Captain in the army and was soon to be transferred to Cairns. A third cousin, on Dad's side, was in the army. At six feet eight inches (200cms) he was reputed to be the tallest man in the A.I.F.. His height was almost his undoing. In a scuffle to seek shelter in a Middle Eastern trench, someone hurtled on top of him as he crouched there resulted in damaged vertebrae and a long stint in hospital.

With no brothers, Jean and I adopted our cousins, writing to them and sending them parcels when we could – though it was Mum who baked the fruit cakes sent for Christmas. At first, the land war was limited to Europe, although the

---

8 *Courier Mail, Brisbane. 4th Sept. 1939*

oceans were scenes of death and danger. Bombers decimated English cities and in retaliation, German cities and citizens were also bombed. Many civilians were killed, their homes and many centuries-old buildings destroyed on both sides. At school, our Domestic Science classes were taken up with sewing and cooking. The sewing was under a special scheme 'Clothes for Bomb Victims', British only, of course. Material, which had mostly to be imported was in short supply but the Education Department managed to get hold of rolls of an uninteresting grey flannel. We were each issued with enough of the fabric to make a skirt (straight, no flare or pleats and with a buttoned placket) and a sleeveless vest with three buttons and 'bound' buttonholes down the front. Teacher helped each girl draft the pattern to her own measurements and we set to work to make these outfits. They would be sent to the Bomb Victims. To relieve the dreariness of the humdrum grey, Teacher suggested we embroider in bright colours a design of our choice on a little breast-pocket she added to the design of the vest. I put a lovely red (chestnut) horse's head on mine.

Unfortunately, there was a shortage of sewing machines too. The ones we did have at Domestic Science were the old treadle, foot-propelled ones. I don't think that even Teacher had an electrically-powered one. Many of the seams had to be done by hand and unfortunately the little outfits took longer to make than we'd envisaged. Some of the models had grown, so that the resulting effect was of a very tight fit. Finally, the day came when a School Inspector came to evaluate our work and to pack our gifts in big wooden boxes, ready to be shipped to the Bomb Victims on the first available boat. We were all rather chuffed but I wished I hadn't heard the Inspector's remark to the teacher as she folded my skirt and vest with its horsehead pocket, 'I hope a bomb doesn't drop too close to the child wearing this. It'll come apart.' I know my hand-sewing wasn't the neatest in the class. Gran said my stitches were the 'homeward bound' kind, getting longer and longer as I progressed but – there was no need for that comment. I'd hoped to hear a nice word for my horse's head. Many girls enclosed little notes with their addresses in the pocket of their gift. I crumpled mine up when I overheard the Inspector's comment but slipped in the new crochet-edged hanky Gran had given me.

The war still seemed a long way away although we felt for the families in the bombed cities. Many children were evacuated from the bombed zones. Some went to Canada, some to Australia. The King, George VI, was asked to consider evacuating the Queen and the two princesses to safety but he declined saying that he asked for no preferential treatment. Most Londoners stayed put. Princess Elizabeth, now the Queen, learnt to drive and became an Ambulance driver in London. But it was here, in Australia, in little Tully, that one of the biggest bombs dropped.

Hurried Internments

Constables Kimlin and Tapsell were aghast. They had received orders to detain an enemy alien destined for internment in the South. It was their mate, Rudi, and they had no choice but to go out to the farm and apprehend him. Tapsell told Dad that the final straw for him was when they loaded Rudi and his small case into the car, little Katherine sat pretending to read from a *North Queensland Register*, 'Poor Bubba got no Dadda,' over and over again. Rudi had been in the German Airforce in World War1 and had told us how he'd spent most of his time in an Italian prisoner-of-war camp. Very early in the piece, his plane had been forced down in an Italian potato field and, as the Italians were on our side in that war, he was taken prisoner. We'd thought nothing sinister of it.

Dad and the two policemen couldn't find any logical reason for Rudi's internment. He was certainly pleased to be living in Australia and the work he did greatly benefited the mill, and through it, the community. But it was here that they thought they may have found a clue. Rudi was a perfectionist. Anything he did had to be faultless, so much so that he had on occasion sent back inferior work done by the engineering workers to be rectified and up-graded. This, in our world of 'That'll do,' probably made him an enemy. At that stage, a name was all that the Government requested to intern an 'alien'. They needed no evidence of subversion. When the three friends reached this conclusion, they felt a little relieved. They each wrote a letter with a glowing character reference for Rudi to the Department head, confident that it would not be long before Rudi was back with his family and friends, completely exonerated. They were wrong. The Department had more urgent things to do and Rudi wasn't released until the end of the war. Conditions for future internments were amended though and no one was apprehended without proof of sedition, but that didn't help Rudi.

Meanwhile, it was painful to see the alarm, anxiety and uneasiness in children of Italian descent at school. This time Italy, under Mussolini, had allied with Hitler and Germany. Some of the children in my class had big brothers in the Australian Army. They were completely Australian, born here, but some fathers, so much at home in their new country, had neglected to take out Australian citizenship or 'naturalisation'. It was our little bit of tragedy in the heartbreak and catastrophe of war.

Move to the Farm

There was a follow-up to Rudi's internment. The acreage where the family was living was owned by an old German. Perhaps his papers, too, were out of order, but he panicked, thinking that he might be next. He told Irene she had to pack up and leave. She did have Greek relations in the district but the distraught old man gave her no time to make arrangements. Fortunately Rudi's mates were still in touch and came to the rescue. Dad was told of a farm of about today's fifty hectares for sale also on Jarrah Creek Road, but a little closer to town. The asking price was about the same as his annual salary, near the valuation of my violin, 350 pounds ($700). As quickly as he could, he got together enough finance to secure delivery and sealed the deal. All hands helped Irene move herself, her family and their possessions without delay.

The farm had been an old tropical fruit farm, abandoned because of the distance from markets and with not enough rainfall or soil fertility for sugarcane. We sometimes found tiny little pineapples along the trunks of fallen logs, about small orange size but rather sweet. By the spring were bananas that looked as if they too had survived. They were a step ahead of the wild plants.

The house, though basic, was a palace compared to the one the family was forced to leave. It was on low blocks, with a big central room enclosed on three sides by a verandah, so that it looked like an unfinished half of a house. Even the roof gave the impression that another half was yet to be added. The verandah in front had a half-wall, one corner was an enclosed bathroom (without a bath) and the back verandah was closed-in to make a kitchen/dining room. A stove recess for the wood-burning stove jutted out from the kitchen end under a lean-to roof that also housed the laundry, a bench and a round iron washtub. There was, of course, no power, no phone, no reticulated water or any of the usual amenities.

Near the house was a small shed, a fowl-yard and a cow-bail. There were a few useless odds and ends left abandoned in the shed and we children loved fossicking through them and wondering what they could be used for. That is, until Bub nearly caused a major calamity. We found some shiny silver capsules in a tin. Unknown to us older ones, Bub souvenired one, thinking it might be a lolly and tried to chew it with her tiny baby teeth. Thankfully, the metal was too rigid and her bite had little effect. Showing the damaged item to Irene for identification, we weren't in the slightest prepared for her reaction. She nearly had a fit. It was a detonator, to be used with explosives for blasting. Had Bub been successful in crunching her silver 'lolly', she could've blown her head off. My father was also present and his response was equally intemperate for a few minutes. He had recently lost an eye when an elderly (and half-blind) driver had knocked him down. In its place he wore a glass eye in the empty socket. After delivery a lecture on safety, he removed his eye and left it on a cupboard to watch us while he went back to his work. It did have a restraining effect on the little ones and we weren't too happy about that eerie eye watching us either.

The loss of his eye had considerable effect on his vision, Dad was not at all prepared with the changes it brought about. He seemed to have lost all sense of distance. His tennis and golf suffered when he couldn't judge where to hit the ball. He'd take a swipe – and miss. The saddest thing, and one none of us could understand, was how it affected his shooting ability. You only needed one eye to sight-up the target but that one eye didn't seem to work for Dad anymore either. We gradually took over as turkey-providers.

Being closer to school than previously and with a slightly shorter bike ride to town each week day, carrying schoolbags and doubling one of the littlies, Charlie and Theresa found themselves with a little bit more free time. They were without their father and breadwinner and with the children to look after, Irene couldn't take a regular job, but their friends rallied and the family managed to survive. The first year, the German Red Cross sent Irene a food parcel, complete with one or two bottles of vitamin tablets. Her warm, Mediterranean temperament almost exploded with indignation. There were no more parcels and the family took their vitamins from home-grown vegetables, fruit and farm produce.

About this time, Mum went to Sydney to visit her sisters. Aunt Jean, twenty years Mum's senior, was very excited about women being sought for work as welders and rivetters in the shipyards. Well into her sixties, she was turned down, but she considered that her young sister would be ideal for the job and could contribute to the War Effort. Dad and I couldn't see Mum as a rivetter despite her burning patriotism. Gran didn't voice an opinion. I think she would have liked to have been able to try it. In any case, it was a good excuse for Mum to pack her ports and take the train to Sydney. The problem was that, when she decided to return home, the rail was far too important to the War Effort to be used by civilians and Mum found herself stranded in Sydney. The risk of war on our mainland was beginning to be more than a nasty threat.

Japan Enters the War

The Japanese forces were getting closer. Pearl Harbour was savagely attacked by the their airforce in late 1941 and the Americans, having lost many of their naval vessels there, entered the war on the side of the Allies and the Australian Prime Minister, John Curtin, declared war on Japan. Japanese forces advanced further south. Darwin was bombed as was Townsville but here the only casualty was an unfortunate Air Raid warden who had his arm broken in a collision with an American jeep. Midget Jap submarines cannily entered Sydney Harbour and sunk the *Kuttabul.* Singapore fell and fifteen thousand Australian soldiers, mostly from the Eighth Division were taken prisoner. It was serious and rather frightening. All this spread fears that 'someone' was using an illegal radio to send information to the enemy. Spy hunts were common but very few spies were uncovered.

By this time, Charlie had taken over from Rudi as turkey provider. With Mum away, I spent more time at the farm. Dad and Gran visited regularly coming out on Dad's half-day off during the week and returning again after his Saturday morning stint for the weekend. Theresa and I were allowed to go with Charlie when he took Pluto (and Winkie on his days off) shooting. We were only eleven or twelve but were very well trained in the use of fire-arms. My namesake, Len Camplin, was killed after he jumped from a dinghy with a loaded shot-gun at the Pigeon Ground on the Endeavour River at Cooktown. The gun discharged, blowing away the big artery under his armpit and he bled to death before his mates could row him back to Cooktown. Dad took it hard as he and Len were especially good mates and he made sure we handled guns appropriately. Never point a gun at anyone. Don't load until you're ready to aim. Check your gun to see it's empty when you've finished. Never carry a gun while you're getting through a fence. Slide it under first with the barrel pointing away. We knew if we didn't follow the rules, our shooting days would end. Doubtless Mum would not have approved but Irene, an excellent shot herself, had confidence in us.

Charlie and I were big enough to hold the gun with the butt pressed into our shoulders but Theresa's arms were too short. Irene had the same trouble. They used to tuck the rifle stock under their armpit and just sight along the barrel. Despite the unorthodox method, the pair of them rarely missed their target. Turkey still figured prominently on the menu.

We Find a Spy

On one of our after-school forays in the scrub behind the farm, we suddenly came onto a small shelter camouflaged with bough roof and walls. We stopped in our tracks but quickly turned-tail and ran when a rather temperamental Italian neighbour ran at us waving what we thought was a gun. We couldn't get home – turkeyless - quick enough. In volatility, Irene's temperament resembled that of the neighbour's. She headed along the road to the next-door house, steam almost billowing from her ears. The neighbour's wife, a pleasant, friendly woman, soon calmed us all down. It wouldn't be a gun. Gino had sprained his ankle and was walking with a stick. He might have waved his stick at us when we startled him. Somewhat appeased, Irene and her retinue returned home. We weren't entirely convinced. Mrs. G. hadn't said what the bough humpy was for. At that time, Italy was still part of Germany's Axis and we weren't convinced that all was well. There was a hidden radio there for sure.

I desperately wanted Dad and his Police mates to investigate. They didn't take it seriously, had more pressing things to do, and tried to let the matter drop. But I wouldn't give in. Finally, we persuaded Dad to come with us and see this mysterious bough shed. We held our breath as we waited obediently at a safe distance while he went to investigate. No radio. A little grey Fergie tractor and two drums, presumably of fuel.

Because of the shortages caused by the war, tractors with other machinery and fuel, were in short supply so they were all called in to a 'tractor pool' from which tractors could be taken out by all farmers when needed. Petrol, like many other things, was rationed and was only available with the official tickets – and the cash. Dad told Gino that the tractor would have to go into the Pool. Gino objected violently and named two cane-farmers, an Irishman and another Italian, whom he wouldn't allow drive his precious tractor. They never checked the oil or did even minor routine maintenance. Dad's tactful diplomacy came to the fore. He explained to Gino that the tractor must go into the pool but - he would put an annotation besides its listing to say that it was only to be taken out if Gino was the operator. That satisfied the fiery Sicilian, the Fergie went into the pool and Gino was given the bonus of an extra occasional day's wages. All's well that ends well but we hadn't caught our spy.

Things were getting more serious at school also. Our parade ground was dug up and enough 'slit trenches' were made to house all the pupils. Even one tennis court was sacrificed to trenches. Rationing of material, tea, sugar and butter, was implemented and most things were in short supply. Commodities like rice and rubber, which had previously been imported from countries now under Japanese occupation, were things of the past. The threat of German subs stopped the import of goods, like fabrics, previously manufactured in Europe. However, we were all issued with a square of light khaki-coloured material from which we made our own 'air-raid capes'. The cape was roughly circular, tying at the throat, with a hood and two tiny pockets in the lower front corners. Into these went a white rubber clothes peg and a wad of cotton wool. When the bombs started to drop, we were to clamp our teeth on the peg and to plug our ears with the cotton wool. The State Schools must have cornered the market on white rubber pegs. The poor Convent kids had to clamp their teeth on small rectangles of (boiled) car tyre.

We had regular air-raid practice. No one knew when it might begin, but, on hearing the warning siren, we'd hurry from the classroom, kept in order by the teacher and monitors and take our set places in the trenches until the All Clear was sounded. It brought the thought of war closer.

While at the farm one weekend, I had an unscheduled lesson in advanced equitation. Two men rode in and pulled up to talk to Dad. They were later joined by a mate in an old wooden-tray farm ute. They squatted down beside their horses and were soon in earnest conversation about the war and the weather, topics that didn't interest me overmuch. I was more interested in the horses. One, a mare, was so very grey that she was almost milk-white. A real story-book horse. During a lull in the talking, I asked if I could have a ride on her. 'Can you ride?' countered the mare's owner. 'Of course,' and before Dad had a chance to say anything, the man helped me into the saddle. I had intended just to ride around the house to show Charlie and Theresa how I could ride but the mare had other ideas. Catching a glimpse of this small, weird thing on her back she panicked and, despite her owner's effort to restrain her, took off down the road. There had been no time to shorten the stirrup leathers to suit my short legs and the heavy metal stirrup irons banged her ribs on both sides. She'd been taught that a nudge in the ribs meant to liven up, so she obliged. As we careered along the gravel road past the butcher's slaughter yard we were going fast enough to beat the average racehorse.

My main aim was not to fall off but I tried several times, without any luck, to rein her in. At the sharpest corner on our hurried way to town we missed an out-going timber-truck by a hair's breadth and without the mare faltering, but, as we got to the Cemetery gates, for some reason she responded to my frantic tug on the reins. She came to a sudden stop that any Quarter Horse trainer would have envied and I shot out of the saddle to land on the road in front of her. Almost immediately her owner jumped out of the ute that had been in hot pursuit. The mare meekly allowed him to take her dangling reins and his mate lifted me to my shaky feet. I had a great patch of skin abraded from inside my left elbow – the scar stayed for decades – and my left knee was bleeding profusely. Apart from that I was 'all right'. They drove me back while the mare's owner led her from the back of the ute. Everyone was anxiously gathered in front of the house when we pulled up. Assuring himself that there was no great damage done, Dad shortened the mare's stirrups, held her head and told me, 'Get back on her, Possum'. I obeyed and the mare, now quite chastened and contrite, walked slowly off on a dignified circuit of the house. When I got back, Dad helped me dismount. I was very, very stiff but I'd followed the Golden Rule. If you get thrown, get on again and show 'em who's boss.

Air raid practice was still in vogue and though, with my injuries being confined to the left side, I could still do my schoolwork, extra-curricular activities were somewhat curtailed. As my mates ran for the trenches, I hobbled behind, not helped by our teacher, Mr. Lewis, who bellowed continually, 'Get a move on, Hopalong!' It was more of a comment on my lack of speed than any reference to my cowboy hero, Hopalong Cassidy.

Rationing

At about this time, in an attempt to conserve the limited stocks of imported materials the Government introduced 'Fashions for Victory.'[9]Men's suits figured prominently on the list. There were to be no more vests and no more double-breasted coats. Trousers were to be cuff-less with 'bottoms' less than 19 inches (about 50cms) wide. Coats were to be made without belts and 'ornamental'

9 *Courier Mail, Brisbane. 27th July 1942.*

buttons on sleeves were forbidden. Trousers were to be limited to having no more than three pockets. Women's clothing fared just as badly. Skirts must not have 'excessive fullness', nor be overly long. 'Shirring, tucking and pleating' must be reduced to a minimum and 'dolman, balloon and leg-of-mutton sleeves' were 'out'. As for men, buttons were only acceptable if functional (with a maximum of five buttons and two pockets per costume) and for everyone, evening frocks, riding breeches and ski-wear were not to be manufactured. On the underwear front, 'bloomers' with elastic at waist and legs were to be replaced by 'panties' with elastic only at the waistline. For children, 'party and speech night frocks' were 'out' but school tunics could still retain their double-material yokes. The restrictions were imposed by the Minister for War Organisation of Industry, Mr. Dedman.

During the year, two women visited the school, taking the height and weight of all pupils. They returned some months later and repeated their measurements. Any children who had grown at a rate considered over the norm, received a small extra issue of clothing coupons. I was lucky enough to score. Brides also received a coupon allowance to buy linen for their homes (not frivolous wedding dresses) – even tea-towels cost coupons – and new mothers received a small amount for baby's layette. When it was realised that parcels, especially cakes, wrapped in paper and sent to the troops, were often damaged in transit, squares of coupon-free unbleached calico were made available for wrapping. These were avidly pounced upon by women who made underclothes (even bras), pyjamas, aprons and other useful items from them. Flour also came in cotton bags and these were saved and used by thrifty home-needlewomen.

When Mr. Irish, the school Principal, moved into his new school, he caused a bit of argument over his decision to have large rose-gardens between the school steps and the gate but his foresight paid off. The roses grew superbly and some of us were detailed each school morning to pick bunches of the roses and deliver them to fulfill orders from the nearby houses, mainly mill employee's residences. The ladies would order what they required and pay us on delivery. I think it was one shilling and sixpence (15c) a bunch of about a dozen roses and the money went as a school donation to the Red Cross and the Comforts Fund. We had varying project clubs, the Poultry Club, Improved Pasture, sponsored by Brice Henry who pioneered 'improved pasture' for cattle in the district, Gardening and Forestry. The Poultry Club produced eggs, and sometimes reject fowls, for sale while the Gardening Club, as well as vegetables for sale, produced buckets of rosellas from which the Domestic Science girls made bottles of readily-marketed jam. The Forestry was a longer-term project and the trees hadn't grown to anywhere near millable size. We had to measure and record their growth regularly at 'breast height'. The boys weren't at all happy about that. It should have been 'chest height'.

Helping 'Our Brave Boys'

About this time, our local baker and the town's mover and shaker, Violet Smith, formed a Junior Red Cross association. We met at the baker shop weekly and were treated to hot buns after our time spent in learning to do new things. We learnt bandaging and elementary first-aid and how to knit scarves and patches for quilts for our 'brave boys' in the Services. For a while some boys joined us but the knitting turned them off the idea. Some children could master the tricky four, double-pointed needles and knitted socks, but, fortunately Smithy didn't expect us all to be that clever. We helped make camouflage nets (the boys enjoyed that part). These were made to be thrown over gun emplacements to hide them from enemy aircraft and we felt very important indeed when working on them. Dad knew all about nets and netting, having made his own cast- and drag-nets and made light, wooden spool-needles for us to use in our net-making. One of the things we liked doing best was making crossword puzzle cards for 'our brave boys in hospital'. Very little was discarded in those days of shortages and we collected crosswords and their answers from wherever they could be found. Cardboard was saved from the backs of writing pads (also in short supply) and short pencil ends that might, in normal times, have been thrown out. The puzzle was glued (with flour and water paste) onto one side of the card with the answers pasted onto the back. String and pretty pictures were also collected and the pencil stubs were attached by string to the card, which, as a final artistic gesture, was decorated with a suitable picture. They must've been appreciated as Smithy received thank-you letters on our behalf. We also helped (or hindered) her as she made dozens of fruit cakes in her baker's oven. These would go to the 'boys' on active service.

Another exciting thing happened when Mum's nephew, my cousin Phil, got in touch from Cairns to see if he and his driver could camp overnight at our place. Very few people had telephones in their homes. Letters were the main form of communication with telegrams, delivered by a telegram boy on a push-bike, for emergencies. Phil sent a telegram, Mum hurried to send one back and, in due course, Phil arrived with his driver in a big, ungainly blitz truck called 'Bombo'. Mum, not long back from seeing Phil's mother in Sydney, was overjoyed and Phil did look smart in his Captain's uniform. They were to drive to Cardwell on a secret mission. I badly wanted to ride in Bombo and offered to go with them to show them the way. Phil agreed with a smile, knowing full well that there was only one road to Cardwell – and back. He and his driver had Army rations but Mum insisted on supplying us with dainty sandwiches and her special scones.

It was a slow trip. At every bridge, whether road- or rail-, they stopped and Paddy, the driver, drilled a hole into one or more of the beams. Phil checked them, then sealed the openings. It was all very mysterious and the trip took us all day. That night, I overheard the grown-ups talking. The holes were for dynamite that would be inserted and detonated should the Japanese Army arrive.

Mum was ecstatic over her handsome nephew's visit and was over-the-mon when he got in touch again to see if he could bring his Commanding Officer down. This time, they left Bombo in Cairns and brought a smaller all-terrain vehicle. On arrival, the Colonel seemed very taken with the view from the verandah so Mum set up the folding card-table with its crocheted cloth and all her usual goodies, on the verandah. Her pride turned to utter disillusionment and horror when, looking townwards over the white railings, the Colonel said, 'You're right, Captain. If we mounted a gun here, we'd be able to control all north and south traffic.'

Mum's previous delight deflated like a punctured balloon. They didn't need to install their gun, however. The navy repelled the would-be invaders at the Battle of the Coral Sea but Phil ceased to be my mother's favourite nephew after that short episode. For a while, I collected old toothbrushes for Paddy. He was an exponent of 'trench art'. There were periods, even in a war, of no planned activity. To fill in the time imaginative men created works of art from materials at hand. Paddy made rings using scrap, silver-coloured metal from pieces of airplane wings. Set into the rings were the regimental colours of the different companies of men. This was where the brightly coloured toothbrush handles came in. They provided the material for the colour patches. Paddy wanted black for a red and black colour patch but that was one I wasn't able to provide. Some soldiers used the toothbrush handles as carving material. Three-oh-three rifles were a favourite and were carved in amazing detail from the old handle.

Inspector's Visit And The School Closes

At school, the Inspector still made his rounds. Our teacher, Miss Dobe, eager to make a good impression put us through a dress rehearsal. In our class of eleven and twelve year olds was a boy, Billy Kirwan, who was fourteen. Billy had no mother and lived with his father a few miles past the farm. As his father's off-sider there was nothing Billy couldn't do. He made excellent bridles and whips and his tin-smithing even stretched to the most workmanlike billy cans and pannikins but he didn't see any sense in school and book-learning. At fourteen he was legally able to leave school (he had hopes of putting his age up and enlisting in the Army) but Miss Dobe made his leaving conditional. He had to learn the two-times multiplication table. Once that was accomplished, he could leave with her blessing.

Miss Dobe explained to us what would happen when the Inspector arrived. As he entered we would all stand up and say 'Good morning, Sir'. He would reply with a 'Good morning, children,' and tell us to sit. Then he would probably select one child who would stand. Miss Dobe, at random, pointed to one of the girls and indicated that she should stand. As Inspector, Miss Dobe asked, 'And what is your name?' 'Milly Paperone, Miss,' Milly answered, wondering what Miss Dobe was getting at. 'Sir', Miss Dobe said. 'I am showing you what the Inspector will do. Now, Millie, he will probably ask you a question or two and then tell you to be seated again. When he leaves, you will all rise and politely say 'Good day, Sir'. Now, do you all know what to do?' Yes, we understood perfectly. It was unfortunate that it was Billy whom the Inspector selected for questioning. But Billy had learnt the instructions well. When asked his name he didn't make Milly's early mistake but confidently replied, 'Milly Paparone, Sir.' Miss Dobe's normally ash-white face glowed red and we all sympathised. Later, when the Inspector visited the Manual Training room, the teacher there was confused when the Inspector, after admiring various pieces of tin, wood and leather, announced 'My word, that Billy Paparone is talented.' Eventually, Billy did leave school.

While the invasion still threatened, the coastal schools closed. Many people had already left for the South and I guess the Government didn't want to take the responsibility of having so many children in the one vulnerable place. I was sent to join Jean at Blackheath in Charters Towers.

Charters Towers Days

It was rather exciting travelling to Townsville with a friend of my parents. Of course, I thought myself quite an expert on the country we traversed by train and, I think in retrospect, could have irritated my minder more than a little. She was trying to read a book. She put me on the train to the Towers where someone from Blackheath picked up two Townsville girls and me and took us to our dormitory at Blackheath. I knew a couple of Jean's friends but senior girls rarely deigned to notice 'babies'. One of the Townsville girls, Claudia, was in the same grade as I was and we became good friends.

War Tragedies too Close to Home

February, 1942, was a very sad start to the year for a girl who was to become my classmate and friend for the next three terms. Barbara's parents worked on a Presbyterian Mission on one of the islands out from Darwin and the church had offered to take her as a boarder at Blackheath, at least until things settled down. Barbara's father was a teacher on the island, her mother, a nurse. In that capacity she was in Darwin to get fresh medical supplies when the angry cloud of twin-engined Japanese bombers came over. She was sitting in the doctor's room with her back to the window, facing him across the desk. The window was directly opposite the Post Office. It suffered a direct hit. Flying masonry struck Barbara's mother causing severe head and other injuries. The authorities tried to evacuate the wounded by road convoy to Townsville, the closest big hospital, but Barbara's mother didn't make it.

It was heartbreakingly sad to see Barbara's grief, knowing how little any of us could do to assuage it. Had her father been closer it would surely have helped but there was a war on. Civilian travel was extremely limited. Her sorrow brought home to us as nothing else could, the futility and the senseless cruelty of war.

There were, of course, good times. The school was putting on a play, *The Boy David,* in which Jean was playing the leading part and I was given a 'bit' – and a very small bit – part. I came on stage and said four words. At least I had no trouble in learning my lines. The rehearsals were great fun but I wasn't there for the opening Night. When the coastal schools re-opened their doors I returned to Tully, only a few weeks before the play was to be presented and caused me possibly the only pang of regret that I couldn't stay for the full year. At least it didn't take my understudy long to learn my line.

U.S. Forces at Charters Towers

We had American troops all around us. They had taken over some of the church boarding schools completely. One girls' school transferred its boarders out west to Richmond and a boys' college, taken over as a hospital, re-located for a while on the banks of the Burdekin River. Blackheath and its brother school, Thornburgh, were comparatively fortunate. There were U.S. personnel camped on the sports ground at Thornburgh and, understandably, the boys were more than a little unhappy as it meant an early end to both the footie and the cricket seasons. There were big guns on the encampment and unfortunately no-one had thought of the damage they would do when they were routinely fired. The main school buildings dated from Charters Towers' gold-rush glory days and had ornate, plaster ceilings. Firing the field guns resulted in great hunks of plaster grapes and grapevines plummeting down from these high ceilings. Gun practice was somewhat curtailed after that episode.

At Blackheath, our sports-ground was on the other side of the street to the residential college houses (we did school with the boys at Thornburgh). Lining the sports-ground side of the street was an avenue of the beautiful shady fig-trees for which the Towers was noted. An ideal place to camp, and a tent town of American servicemen soon sprang up in a line under the trees. We had to pass through a small space in the row to get to the sports-ground after school.

Barbara and I were more interested in reading than in sports, played in tops and elastic-legged bloomers that wouldn't have met Mr. Dedman's Victory standards. There was an old orchard, with small but sweet oranges, next to the sports-ground and we often disappeared there through an old paling fence with our Townsville mate, Claudia. Jean used it for a retreat, too, until a foraging Charters Towers goat began chewing one of her long pigtails as she lent back against the palings, blissfully reading her book. The goat took quite a few inches from the end of her plait. It was here, in the orchard, that we met Johnnie. He was a U.S. airman and, we thought, rather homesick. We often met him there and downed our books to talk to him and to share the oranges he'd scrounged. He had a kid sister about our age, he told us, and kindly kept us supplied with chewing gum and the occasional chocolate. These were luxuries that weren't to be found any more in Australian shops since the early days of the war. He was a rear-gunner in a plane called Kalamazoo Kate. Like most of the planes it had a pin-up girl (Kate?) painted on its fusilage.

There was an elevated walkway that bridged the space between the two dormitory buildings. We usually crossed it on our way to the dining room, just as the bombers flew over on the way to their targets much further north. It was not far from the airstrip so they were still flying low enough for us to identify some of our favourite planes by their pin-ups. They returned not long after daylight as we went to breakfast so that we could count them and breathe a relieved sigh when Kalamazoo Kate flew past. One morning Kate was flying awkwardly and lower than the others, a good way behind on her own. We were aghast. Kalamazoo Kate's tail was just about non-existent. She had been badly damaged.

We had seen Johnnie the afternoon before he left on that mission and he took three little metal badges from his cap and pressed them into our hands. Mine was a Fort Worth badge and I treasured it for years. It didn't help at all when we overheard the kitchen staff discussing the raid. Two bombers failed to return and one of the maids was excitedly telling how Kalamazoo Kate was such a mess 'they had to hose out all the blood and stuff.' The three of us left. We never saw Johnnie again.

If you wanted to know anything about what was going on you had only to ask one of the domestics. They had all the information about the progress of the war, any military goings-on and all the local scandals. Most of them dated the Yanks who kept them well supplied with, apart from a dashing escort dressed in a uniform of much better cut and quality than its Australian equivalent, nylon stockings, lipstick and other treats. Stockings worn by Australian women before the war were either silk (for best wear) or thicker lisle for everyday use. Some American invented the man-made nylon, which, made into stockings, was a huge success. Stockings, like double-breasted coats, elasticised bloomer-legs and men's trouser cuffs were not to be manufactured in Australia. Some inventive person came out with a beige-y coloured liquid that was smeared on the bare legs to look like a stocking. A rear seam applied with an eyebrow pencil to the dried paint completed the illusion of stocking-clad legs. Nylons, however, were so much easier to put on and looked doubly seductive. An American boyfriend was something to be desired and not only for the pleasure of his company and the status it brought with it. The Australian servicemen weren't filled with the same admiration for the G.Is that the girls had. The Yanks, with their much higher pay, better-fitting uniforms and superfluity of gifts were a bit too popular. As one put it, they were 'over paid, over sexed and over here.' Fortunately, when it got down to the business of war, with no civilian women involved, they got on and fought well together, truly allies.

A Marbles Professional

As in Tully and the townships all over Australia, fetes, raffles, dances and other fund-raisers were forever being held to help the Red Cross and other support agencies. Thornburgh often hosted garden-party fetes with the servicemen competing against the schoolboys in some sporting action. Claudia and I were doing our rounds when we came across two boys from our class playing marbles, shooting them out of a ring drawn on the ground. A small group of American G.Is were encouraging them. We pulled up to watch and before I could escape, one of the Yanks pressed some marbles into my hand with a cheery, 'Here, you shoot for me, Kid.' I was too surprised to object so squatted down to try to get rid of my boy opponent's marbles before he eradicated mine. The Americans were betting on the outcome, pulling out two-shilling coins (20c). The two shillings was officially called a 'florin', a title that was engraved on it. The American, not too familiar with Australian currency, picked one out and, reading its name, said, 'I bet one flor-in.' 'Up you a flor-in,' countered his mate and they put the two coins at the side of the ring. My fellow contestant, obviously ill at ease at playing with a girl, muffed a couple of shots and I hit his marbles out of the ring. I'd won. The American clapped me on the back and presented me with the two two-shilling pieces. I didn't know what to do but Claudia whispered 'Keep them'. I did. I was rich beyond my wildest dreams. Pocket-money was usually sixpence (5c) a week.

As the afternoon went on I made plans for spending my wealth. As a school we used to walk everywhere – no fuel for buses – in a 'crocodile', a long line of girls walking two abreast, the senior classes in the lead and the 'babies' at the end. Each day we walked to Thornburgh for school. Our classes were co-educational with the boys. After school we lined up and walked back to Blackheath. Even on Sundays, the crocodile came out again to get us to church. We alternated Methodist services with those at the Presbyterian church and the route took us through town. In one of the shop windows was a Kodak box-Brownie camera. I'd had my eye on it for ages. Dad had been a keen photographer and had wonderful albums of war photos taken by a mate and another one of photos he'd taken of the amazing limestone caves at Chillagoe. I wanted that camera to take my own photos. It was six shillings (60c) With a bit of luck I could rake up the other two shillings. Gran sometimes sent me postal notes for that amount and Jean might lend me the necessary if I couldn't make the full amount. Jean did lend me the last sixpence (5c) conditional to being able to borrow the camera. All I had to do was to get a sympathetic kitchen maid to buy it for me. They were kind-hearted and often helped out. A day or two after raising the money I had my camera. My euphoric dreams were soon shattered. It was wartime. There were no films available. It was years before I was able to try out my prize.

While our meals were as tasty and as nutritious as was possible, there were no extras. The Yanks had stacks of ice cream, but we had none. Even the cases of fruit, apples from Stanthorpe and tropical fruit from home, that parents had traditionally railed regularly to their children, failed to arrive, or if they did, were well past their use-by date when they did turn up. The armed forces had priority in the way of transport and the Americans seemed always to have first priority. If you weren't fortunate enough to have an American friend it could cause resentment.

Exit the Mill Chimney

Once, on Saturday mornings, a tuckshop used to open at Blackheath where you could use your pocket-money to buy ice creams, ice blocks, lollies or fruit. That was now a thing of the past. There was nothing to put in a tuckshop. Saturday morning was also hair-washing time. After breakfast we washed our hair, usually long and plaited, and sat in the sun for it to dry. On one particular Saturday we hurriedly found something to sit on and took up our positions, towels over our shoulders, facing Towers Hill, waiting. The kitchen staff had the inside information that, at nine o'clock, the Americans were going to blow up (or blow down) the gigantic brick chimney stack, a reminder of Charters Towers' golden days, on top of Towers Hill. It was considered too easy a landmark to be picked up by Japanese navigators to confirm their bearings as they flew down from New Guinea. It was also thought to be a hazard to homing Allied planes. We waited and waited. Nothing happened. Then, just as we'd given up and were getting ready to go in for lunch, there was an enormous explosion. The top of the hill near where the tower had stood was enveloped in an almost impenetrable cloud but we were sure we could detect the path of individual bricks as they soared high in their mad career before plunging back to earth. It was a breath-taking experience and really made our usually pretty colourless day. We talked about it for weeks.

Years later I recalled the experience when talking to an older man with a war-service background. I told how we'd just about given up waiting, the detonation was so late in coming. It was supposed to be blown down much earlier. At first, he was silent and disapproving, then, rather savagely, 'How did you know when it was to go up? It was a military secret!' That only confirmed something we all knew. If you wanted to hear what was happening around the place, ask a kitchen maid. Their information was all-compassing and accurate. They knew it all.

There were Australians stationed around the Towers but the Americans seemed to greatly out-number them. It was a pleasant surprise one evening to see one of our old Tully teachers, a general favourite, Mr. Lewis, turn up at the school in Airforce uniform. He was dating one of the junior mistresses and called several times before, apparently, being posted further north. They were both from the Atherton Tableland.

A favourite with everyone was the American Padre, Lieutenant (pronounced Loo- ten-ant) Logan. He often preached at the local churches and occasionally came to the schools. Leffy Logan radiated nothing but charm and goodwill. When the threat of invasion was at its highest, when we'd all lost people we had known and loved, and when life looked very dark, Leffy preached a sermon on faith. He told us that we must have faith and quoted from the Bible, 'Faith is the substance of things hoped for, the evidence of things not seen'. If we only had faith we could be sure that everything would work out for the best. He sounded so sincere and so convincing that we all went home feeling much more confident about the war's outcome. Sixty years later, when sister Jean visited me, the conversation swung around to Leffy Logan. 'Do you remember that sermon he preached on faith?' she asked. As if on cue we both began to quote Hebrews 11 word for word. As our knowledge of the bible was pretty well limited to 'The Lord is my shepherd…' we were both absolutely astounded. Leffy Logan sure had charisma.

Eventually the coastal schools re-opened and I returned home to Tully. After I left, Jean had a rather scary experience in the Towers. She'd been spending a 'free' weekend with the family of one of Dad's friends. Just as the father was getting ready to take Jean back to Blackheath, one of the younger children who had been flushed and running a bit of a temperature all day, suddenly developed alarming symptoms and looked as if she were about to convulse. The Doctor was called but was slow to respond. The whole family was frantic. Jean was only slightly less so and, if she didn't get back before the evening 'deadline,' she'd be 'gated'. No leave passes given.

An Eerie Encounter in the Park

When she offered to walk the few blocks back to school, her friends, not seeing any danger in her suggestion, and with their thoughts thoroughly centred on the little one, sent her on her way with heartfelt thanks. It wasn't yet dark so Jean decided to take a diagonal course, a short-cut through the Park. She had only been in the park for a few minutes when the strangest feeling came over her. She found she was shivering, despite the tropical heat and couldn't take a step forward. Her feet stubbornly refused to move ahead. With increasing feelings of there being something wrong, she panicked and spun around. Movement in that direction was possible and she raced back out to the road to return to school 'the long way'. On arrival, she was still nervy and on edge, a fact not missed by the teacher who signed her in. She was most disapproving of Jean walking home alone although Jean was careful not to say a word about the Park or her eerie experience there.

Next morning, still feeling not totally recovered, she was summoned to the Head's office to be confronted by two policemen. At first she just mentioned walking home but, when one of the policemen pointedly asked had she come through the Park, the weird story came tumbling out. The policemen asked had she heard anything that would have frightened her, caused her panic? She told them 'no' and stressed that it was deathly quiet, no sound at all, not even the slightest of the usual natural noises of the night. The police seemed satisfied that she knew nothing more and left but Jean received a stern lecture from the Headmistress for walking home unescorted. She would not be given permission to visit those friends again. She wasn't.

Rumours circulate quickly, especially in a girls' boarding school and the kitchen staff soon supplied the answer to the mystery. At approximately the same time as Jean set foot into the Park a woman had been cruelly strangled by her American lover and left in the bushes besides the path. Jean realised from their description that she was so eerily brought to a halt only inches from the scene. The strangler was apprehended and sentenced. Jean was fearful that she might have been called on as a witness but she'd witnessed nothing, just that unbearable, absolute silence and the unnatural icy chill. The police found enough to go on without questioning her again.

When Claudia, Barbara and I crossed to the sports-ground after school through the encampment under the fig trees we heard few remarks about our charms or lack of, but the senior girls got rather up-tight over comments passed on their individual merits or defects as they made their way through. Jean, with her red hair and freckles, was one of the targets. The younger women teachers who supervised sporting activities also resented the comments and, at times, unwelcome advances. Someone began to circulate a poem printed in the local paper and said to be written by one of the tormentors under the fig trees. The first stanza went:

'Somewhere in Australia where the sun is like a curse
Where each dull day is followed by another slightly worse
Where the brick red dust is thicker than the shifting desert sands
And the white man dreams and wishes for the greener, fairer lands.'[10]

It went on for several verses complaining about the lack of civilised social life in Australia and really got under the skins of the affronted Senior girls. Jean was asked to write a reply. She was sixteen with her seventeenth birthday coming up in November.

10 Both poems were printed in the *North Queensland Register*. The soldier's as 'anon', Jean's as 'a Blackheath schoolgirl'.

'Somewhere in Australia where the Yankees are a curse
(If I wasn't such a lady I could think of something worse)
Where the Yankees' hide is thicker than the brick-red dust they scorn
And the baseball players' howlings wake the roosters up ere dawn.'

She also penned several verses and really let her pique show. Circulated among the students, it came in for a lot of admiring praise, more than had ever before come her way. For a brief period she revelled in her fame until the poem was seen by a teacher. Jean was again summoned to the Head's office. That alone was bad enough, but assembled in the office were several smirking teachers and a 'very composed' young man in an American uniform, one of our fig tree neighbours. Instantly Jean was so embarassed and ashamed she wished she could sink through the floor and out of sight. The American smiled, took a step towards her and shook her hand. He spoke to her but what he said was just a blur. In her agitated state none of it registered but he was undeniably wanting to be friends. All that was clear in her muddled brain was a 'sincere wish' that she'd been less 'clever' and a little more 'considerate'. But other exciting things were happening. Her *faux pas* soon forgotten and she eventually managed to live it down.

In later years Jean told me of a blood-curdling experience she'd had when out in the *Sapphire* with Dad and Benny Barnett. I wasn't able to go possibly as the boarding schools often broke-up at the end of the year ahead of the State schools and I would still have been in school. They had landed at Goold Island again to get water when a plane flew over and jettisoned a bomb. It was probably an American bomber returning from New Guinea with the crew not wanting to try to land in Townsville with an unexploded bomb aboard. Pieces of shrapnel and chips of rock peppered the sea and the beach where they were. Jean had a few tiny cuts on her legs but was totally frightened by the experience. Dad and Benny advised her to say nothing about it. None of them was really hurt and keeping the secret would be her part in the War Effort.

Back to Tully

Things were little changed when I returned home. The war was still going in Europe and to our north. The Junior Red Cross girls continued with their projects and we were encouraged to collect scrap metal as well. Aluminium, as in saucepans, was in particular demand. It was re-cycled as airplane fusilages and wings, apart from other more mundane uses. Old car batteries, discarded toothpaste tubes and copper scraps were also welcome. On certain days, varying-sized heaps of the collected metals were put out on the footpath to be picked up by a small truck that saw them on their way to the factories.

The War Goes On

We also had a 'brown out', not as bad as a black-out, but care was taken that no more lights were used than were necessary so that a display of bright lights wouldn't attract Japanese bombers to our town. Some people blacked-out their external windows with brown paper and others shatter-proofed them with criss-crossed pasted strips of rag or paper. Not at all elegant, but it was said to be very effective in preventing the glass from shattering in a bomb blast. Mum reported that, in Sydney, people even papered over the car headlights, leaving only a small circle of about four centimetres diameter uncovered. It made for very careful driving at night., but at least it would be hard for the enemy to see you. Gran knitted faster and longer than ever and women waiting to be seen by doctors or dentists were invited to knit, coloured squares and striped scarves usually, with needles and wool provided along with the more routine out-of-date magazines. One day Dad arrived home with two young British sailors on their way to join their ship in Cairns. Due to some transport hitch they were stranded in Tully, so Dad came to the rescue. Their ship was on the way to the North Sea, up in the Arctic Circle. This worried Gran. Their uniform trousers were navy blue bell-bottoms with very wide flares (that Mr. Dedman would not have approved). Apparently this was a hangover from the days when decks had to be swabbed daily and the wide trouser bottoms readily allowed for the trouser legs to be rolled up and kept dry. However Gran was concerned about the freezing winds of the North Pole. They'd just be funneled up by the bell-bottoms. She immediately abandoned her current knitting and began on a pair of navy blue knee-warmers for each of the boys. The sailors left before they were done but a week or so later Gran received a thank-you note. The knee-warmers (and some Anzac biscuits) arrived in Cairns just in time to catch up with them. The sailors would now be at sea but they would remember her kindly when they reached the icy North Sea and ask Santa to pay Gran a special call when he came south. To make sure, they'd also sent a Christmas card. It came the following Easter.

Dad often brought visitors home but he was quite excited on one occasion. He'd met an old Light Horseman from the 5th Light Horse and would bring him home for lunch the next day. I couldn't work it out. He seemed so enthusiastic about his guest and yet, in all the tales he'd told me of his Light Horse days, the 5th Light Horse and the Camel Corps always featured as 'thieves and robbers'. No horse, gear or item of supplies was safe if the 5th felt that their need was the greater. Scrounging was thought to show initiative and it was a case of anything goes when there's a war to be won. I could not understand Dad inviting a thief and robber into our home but decided to take precautions. I hid my books under a suitcase in the wardrobe. My money box, one of those old metal ones made in the likeness of the Commonwealth Bank, the little china dog Gran gave me and Dad's gift, a slightly larger horse, were carefully wrapped and hidden in the half tank under the reserve of cut stove-wood. To be doubly sure, I tied Winkie up at his home beside the tank.

The thief and robber never showed any signs of piratical leanings and was quite a likeable and entertaining guest. He and Dad recalled their Light Horse days with more emphasis on the good times than the bad while Gran made sure there was tea in the pot and food on the table. Everyone seemed to enjoy the visit so much that I made sure no one was watching as I sneaked up, let Winkie off the chain and surreptitiously returned my treasures to their usual places in my room.

While most goods were in extremely short supply, trades-people still delivered 'orders' of what was available. The grocer delivered by vehicle, as did Violet with her bread, a butcher's boy, like the Post Office's deliverer of telegrams, operated with a bicycle. An exception to the rule were the two Chinese gardeners. Mo Sing came with two baskets cleverly balanced on a slender yoke across his shoulders and Willie Poy had a horse and cart. When the weather was uncomfortably hot, Willie's horse wore a hat, with holes cut for his ears. Willie was the more genial of the two and always tried, at Christmas, to bring some gift for his better customers. Until the war cut off his supply line and his store depleted, it was usually a small jar of ginger preserved in a deliciously tangy syrup.

We Lose Our Gran

Poignantly, not all the sorrow of those years was war-related. One morning, Gran was up at daylight and worried that she couldn't find her 'work'. I went into her room and brought out the khaki socks she was knitting, to be told, 'Not that one. I want my other work.' This was rather out of character. Gran normally would happily accept what you had done for her even if it wasn't quite what she'd had in mind. Dad must've sensed something was wrong and he came into the kitchen. They motioned me outside and, lowering their voices, began a short discussion. From a couple of steps down from the back landing, I could hear, even if I failed to understand. Gran wanted Dad to take her to the hospital. She didn't 'want to be a burden'. Promptly Dad assured her she would never be a burden, made her a cup of tea as the kettle was now boiling and sent me up to feed Gran's chooks. I went to school as usual and tried in vain to put from my mind Gran's desire to get Dr. Unwin to admit her to hospital. She'd begun writing her 'memoirs' at the beginning of the year. Writing pads were hard to come by but Smithy, now the newsagent as well as the baker, found her a thick 240 page exercise book, a little too big for popular school use. Gran's writing was of that very old-fashioned angular kind. I found it extremely hard to read but Dad could de-cypher it. When I was at Blackheath, Gran sometimes sent me a postal note for ' two and six', 25cents, enclosed in a letter. I had no hope of reading it and Jean's skill in that line was very little better. I told Gran not to bother to write any more as I couldn't read her writing. As I grew older I deeply regretted my crass behaviour but now I realise that Gran would only have laughed at her grandchild's infantile failings. She completed her first book and was about a third of the way through a slightly smaller book, bringing her life up to our move to Tully and the start of the war. For the last few weeks much of her knitting time had been given over to memoir writing.

When I came home from school Gran was in her room and had tidied the tiny round table in the corner where she wrote her letters and memoirs. Her ink-bottle was capped, her pen wiped and put in its fancy stand and her two books, one neatly on top of the other, beside them. Gran was just sitting there. She asked if I'd go and collect the eggs and check the chooks' feed and water. They had household scraps mixed with pollard for tea but Gran hadn't boiled the peelings up in the scrap billy as she usually did. I just mixed them raw with the pollard. Dad went in to see Gran as soon as he came home from work and when I arrived back with the day's eggs, I was scarcely allowed to show them to Gran before being sent out to play. The door was shut behind me.

Next day, Gran persuaded both of my parents to contact Dr. Unwin. He called at the house and then went to see Dad at the Court House. When I arrived home from school Dad had already taken Gran to hospital. She died just after eight o'clock that night. My Gran had played such a huge part in my life I could not believe that I would never ever see her again. When I had recovered from my loss sufficiently, I asked Mum where Gran's memoirs were. I badly wanted them. Someday I should be able to read them. I was totally unprepared for Mum's matter-of-fact answer, 'Oh, I burnt all Gran's rubbish.'

I inherited Gran's chooks. When she died my violin lessons stopped so I had plenty of time to check on my poultry each morning before leaving for school – by the short cut again. Gran had two or three regulars who used to buy her eggs. Two shillings (20c) a dozen, I think they were. Egg cartons didn't seem to have been invented and I delivered them in a billycan to the customers. Mum decided it was a good time for me to learn economics and business principles. There are always debits to be considered before a profit is made. I was to pay for the pollard – three or four dozen eggs worth per bag. This cut into my new-found affluence and I objected. Mum took as many eggs as she needed for the house without paying. She countered my objections by saying that she fed me for nothing. I argued that Dad allowed for that in the fortnightly 'house-keeping' money he gave her, but my line of argument was not successful.

There weren't many things in the shops to buy with my egg money so Dad suggested I do my patriotic duty and invest in War Savings Stamps. These were popular with some of the kids at school. A stamp, from memory blue and decorated with a fighter plane, cost six pence (5c) at the Post Office. With it came a card folder with spaces marked for thirty-two stamps. There was quite a bit of competition at school to see who could fill their card first. One stamp a week was considered good going. This could be increased at times like birthdays and Christmases. Once the thirty-two spaces were filled at a total cost of sixteen shillings ($1.60), the card was taken back to the Post Office. In return you were given a certificate to say that in seven years time your investment would be worth one pound ($2) and could be exchanged for that amount at the Post Office. The four shillings (40c) was the seven years' interest that the Government was willing to pay in appreciation of the use of your investment in the War Effort.

Petrol Shortage and Gas Producers

Petrol, which had to be imported, was in very short supply to civilians. It was rigidly rationed. As Clerk of Petty Sessions, Dad was part of a committee of men representing mostly farmers and the sugar mill. In cases of extreme emergency this committee could authorise extra fuel. Fishermen, whose small boats were continually battling uncooperative winds, waves and tides, were also eligible for extra fuel tickets when being stranded was the only alternative.

Strange contrivances, charcoal burners or gas producers, began to appear on some cars. Usually, an apparatus which burnt charcoal was attached or welded to the rear bumper and the 'gas' produced was stored in a balloonlike sac on the car's roof. From there, the gas was somehow taken into the motor as fuel. It did work. The cars drove sedately along the roads but the clouds of stinking black smoke from their exhausts were truly remarkable. Kurt Johannsen, writing in his book *A Son of the Red Centre* tells of the gas-producer he made for his 1928 Studebaker car. He could easily drive a mile on one and a half pounds of wood (approximately, as he wrote, a kilogram per kilometre on a three ton vehicle). The Studebaker could do 8 miles (13k) on the burning of a wooden beer crate made to hold five dozen bottles. He proved it by driving from the Tennant's Creek pub to the Telegraph Station with a top speed of 105km per hour and winning a five pound ($10) bet.

At the farm, we busied ourselves after school heaping scattered wood around the old dry standing stumps and logs. Originally the clearing had been undertaken by ring-barking and much of the dead timber was still in evidence. Dad, Irene and us children had visions of turning into real farmers. Supplies were short and by growing things we could, at least, 'do our bit'. One day Dad brought a new friend to the farm. He was a part-Maori but also answered to the name of Fred (a lot easier to pronounce than his other name). He had been experimenting with growing things we normally imported from southern Asia at a farmlet near Innisfail. However an Army camp had moved in and he and his precious plants were to move to a new home. Our farm fitted the bill and he erected a bough-topped shade house by the spring for his pepper, vanilla,cocoa and other exotic plants. Unfortunately for him, he put some of the hardier plants in a bed behind the house. We could water them for him. It sounded a great idea and we were proud to be able to do our part for the war. That is, until he innocently let it drop that some of these plants were castor oil seedlings. Castor oil was a favoured remedy proposed by Irene and Gran for any number of childhood complaints. We detested it. Even the smell was awful. Somehow, by mistake of course, someone inadvertently emptied the hot ashes direct from the stove's ash-pan onto them. Killed the lot. We were acutely distressed at having to break the sad news to Fred when he came at the week-end. Fortunately, he didn't replace them.

Tragedy struck again when, one evening as we drove home from the farm, there was a small line-up of vehicles at the white railing at the end of the road in front of our house. Dad went over to a group of quietly worried men. They needed his help. He immediately sent us inside and disappeared up the mountain with them. The Mangan boys and their mates had finally made it to the Top Spring. In his exuberance at reaching the wonderful waterfall, Billy went to roll a small rock over the escarpment to celebrate their achievement. He misjudged and went with it. The men needed help to bring his badly battered body home

Bad luck usually happens in threes but this time it almost made it to four. Mum had managed to get a train seat to Sydney again. There was some family mishap and she was needed to help out. It was much easier to acquire a passage south than to get a seat on the north-bound train which was usually given over to the transport of servicemen and their requirements. Dad, Winkie dog and I were home but we usually spent the weekends from Saturday noon when the Court House closed and Wednesday afternoons at the farm. The half-day off during the week balanced the need to work on Saturday mornings. I sometimes spent even more time at the farm, cycling to and from school with the other kids. I'd managed to buy my own bike for 2 pounds ($4). It was before I'd inherited Gran's chooks and raising the money took a bit of hard thought – and work. I cleaned up under our neighbour's high house for 4 shillings (40c) and mowed what seemed like about five acres of lawn for a cane-farmer friend of Dad's for another ten shillings ($1). As it was done with a real 'push' mower with no motor other than me, it took me the best part of a week of the holidays to finish. I did get lovely, fancy patty cakes for smoko, though. Dad kindly 'lent' me a pound ($2) and I had to dig into my lifetime savings for the balance.

Malaria Relapse

Dad hadn't been his usual active self for a day or two and asked me to call at the Court House on my way to school (the 'long way' with the boys now that I had a bike) and tell Jane that he wouldn't be in to work that day. He was lying on the verandah bed when I got back home, was very hot to touch and didn't look anything like his usual happy self. All he wanted to do was to drink water, so I was rather relieved when an unexpected visitor walked up the front steps. It was Jane from the office. She and Dad immediately became involved with a conversation that didn't include me. At the end of it, Jane, who could drive a car, said that she'd take Dad to hospital in our car. This she did, and Dr. Unwin who happened to be there, admitted him immediately. Dad had a severe fever. Jane took me home with her for the night and I went out to the farm with the kids the next day after we'd called to get a progress report from Jane. She had been trying to contact Mum in Sydney and had finally got a message through but – no seats on the train for civilians for some time. Jane tried her best to get Dad's superiors in Brisbane to help but they, too, didn't have much influence in war-time. Dad was out of hospital before Mum was able to make the long, slow train ride back. Dr. Unwin thought that Dad had a relapse of the dreaded malaria.

He had contracted it in the Light Horse when serving around Lake Galilee which was, at that time, rather noted for the fever. After spending weeks in Cairo and Damascus hospitals, he was about to be discharged from the Army because of his ill-health but he recovered sufficiently to go back to his regiment. Here, the war, like his fever, had run its course so he left the Army with the rest of his mates. In the twenty-five years since then, he'd had no sign of the fever until now. Needless to say, we were all acutely worried.

Irene had a job in town and faithfully checked on Dad each day before commencing work. We called in to see him after school and Dr. Unwin was feeling more hopeful about the outcome. Winkie dog still spent the middle of the day at the Court House with Jane who was one of our strongest supporters. She, too, visited the hospital whenever she could. She was a great help to Dad at the Court House and he held her in very high regard. To us, she always looked a little strange. She dressed in pale pastel colours of pink, blue and lemon lystav – a sort of a linen fabric. Mr. Dedman wouldn't have totally approved. Though the skirts were 'straight' and 'sensible', they almost reached Jane's ankles. Her sleeves were long, even on the hottest and most humid summer days and ended in white starched cuffs. The neckline was high and sported a dazzling white 'Peter Pan' collar to match the cuffs. The design never changed. Jane wore it as a uniform. Pinned to the centre of her buttoned bodice was a 'Child of Mary' badge. Its brilliant patina was the first thing you saw when Jane came into view. She had entered a nunnery when she left school and remained there for several years, but when it came to taking the final vows, she had second thoughts and opted out. Her years of training weren't wasted. She was an admirable person and rather ahead of her time in working as assistant at the Court House. Here, she told me proudly, she was paid the same salary as a male clerk, a rather advanced ruling of the Public Service. Women, at that time, were paid less than their male equivalents in most jobs.

As a peace-offering after the tractor affair, Gino's wife presented us one afternoon on the way home from school with a pair of very playful kittens. Irene wasn't especially pleased. A cat to keep mice and snakes away was one thing. Two very lively kittens that regularly got underfoot was another, but we were allowed to keep them.

After he'd been in hospital for over a week, we rode our bikes up to the hospital to see Dad after school, hoping to hear that he could soon leave hospital. We certainly weren't prepared for the sight that assailed us on arrival. He was in a room by himself, with his mosquito net firmly tucked in all around the mattress. When we stood at his bedside – with Winkie dog who always visited – he didn't stir, didn't seem to know we were there. Sweat was pouring from his face and he was making strange and frightening unintelligible noises. At times he'd wildly throw an arm out in any direction. A nurse came in, sponged his face, tidied him as best she could, tried, unsuccessfully, to give him some water and told us to go home. It was getting late and the fever would only take its course. There was no point in hanging about.

We left and were so worried that we didn't notice until we got back to the main part of town that Winkie wasn't with us. Thinking he might have gone on home when the nurse came in and suddenly remembering that Irene had asked us to take the washing in off the line as soon as we arrived home, we kept on going. Irene had just beaten us home and we were very much in disgrace. She raced out to the clothesline in the fading light to get the clothes. As she was busily unpegging, something grabbed her around the ankle. Immediately, blaming the kittens, she tried to kick it away – and then realised that her attacker wasn't soft and furry. Looking down she saw a brown snake.

Snake Bite

In those days, the treatment for snake-bite was to tie a ligature on the limb (between the bite and the heart), cut between the two puncture wounds, suck out any venom (unless you had cavities or infected teeth) and apply Condy's Crystals (permanganate of potash) to the cut. Without a moment's hesitation, Irene got a sharp knife and made the incision in her own leg. I don't know if she or Charlie sucked out the venom but the Condys was applied while Theresa raced down the road to Gino's for help. They immediately came in their ute and conveyed Irene to hospital. We seven kids were left on our own and we realised Winkie dog definitely wasn't there. Did he call at the Court House and stop off with Jane? Too bad. We had other things to think of.

We shut ourselves in the middle room with Pluto, the kittens and the kerosene lamp. Charlie rolled out with Pluto on the floor and, for a start, we all tried to fit in the big double bed. The glass in one of the double doors had a small green pane broken and the lock wouldn't work, so Charlie put one of Irene's tall pot-plant stands against it to hold it shut. Although we were scared stiff and doubly worried now, not only for Dad but for Irene, and knowing that if one snake were seen, its mate was bound to be close by, we went to sleep. But not for long. There was a crash and a bang. Charlie, Theresa and I were immediately alert. The kerosene lamp had nearly burnt itself out but we could see, coming through the missing pane of glass, a sinuous length of snake. Charlie jumped up with our only defence, his tomahawk. Fortunately, he didn't get a chance to use it as, having made it safely through the hole to the pot-plant stand, the second kitten jumped down onto the verandah to join its mate. We all felt rather silly – and acutely relieved. Our 'snake' was the escaping kitten's tail.

It was Saturday, so as soon as we had done the necessary chores, we set off on our bikes, doubling the little ones, for the hospital. What we found certainly compensated for our night of terror. Dad's fever had broken during the night. Dr. Unwin was by his side when he recovered and told him that he'd be able to go home in a day or two, all going well. Dad was very pleased. He'd get a message to Irene and get her to collect a clean set of clothes for him. Dr. Unwin laughed. 'Tell her yourself. She's in the next ward.' He quickly reported on the snake attack and was happy to relate that the emergency treatment had worked. Irene, too, could go home.

We even found Winkie. He'd been with Dad, under his bed, all night. We listened, absolutely fascinated, as Dad told us of his experience. He'd been delirious and the arm-throwing that we'd already noticed was only a start. In his mind he'd been back fighting in the desert. He could hear gunshots and yells and the noises of frightened horses but, eeriest of all, when he thrashed about and struggled, quite wrecking his bedclothes and mosquito net and almost ending on the floor, he could hear the sinister rhythmic beat, beat, beat of an Arab drum. It was infinitely unnerving. As his tossings and turnings increased, he came close to falling out of bed. Half of him was already teetering on the side of the bed-frame when he became conscious of a warm, wet tongue anxiously licking his hand. He reluctantly opened his eyes, not really knowing what he'd find. The riddle of the beating Tom-Tom was solved as a very relieved Winkie came out from under the trailing bedclothes and spiritedly wagged his tail on the ward floor.

Once the fever broke, Dad's recovery was swift and we were able to have both him and Irene back with us. To add to our relief, Mum had managed to get that seat on the north-bound train and arrived, greatly agitated, the evening after. She hadn't heard of Irene's snake bite, so that was one worry that she had been spared. Dad's health, with Mum, Irene and Jane doing all they could to help, very quickly recovered but Mum wasn't happy about remaining in Tully with its resident fever mosquitoes. One of Dad's superiors had been able to help her there. She approached him for a transfer to a drier and more healthy position. Dad, the ardent fisherman, wasn't too pleased when his transfer came through – to Roma, in south-west Queensland.

Transferred Again - To Roma

It took about six months before the time came for us to catch the train south. I'd bought some gladioli corms with my egg-money and had them up and promising beautiful sprays of blossom when Mum arranged for the neighbour to buy them from me for what I'd paid for them. They were only about six inches (15cms) high and quite transplantable. It sounded a practical solution but it was very hard some weeks later to pass the neighbour's garden on the way to school and see the beautiful array of his lemon, scarlet and orange gladioli. But that was nothing compared to Winkie's fate. We were to sell our car again and make the move by train. Winkie couldn't go. For some reason, he couldn't travel with us but had to go on a goods train and there was no one to look after him. His fare to Brisbane and then to Roma wasn't out of the question. I'd sold Gran's chooks and had my gladioli money too. I could manage his fare. A brainwave hit and I wrote to my old music teacher, Mrs. Morton who was now in Rockhampton. Could she meet Winkie, give him a supply of bones and check his water? Knowing Winkie from my violin days, she said she'd be delighted to help. Heartened, I wrote to another friend in Brisbane to ask for the same favour, and, yes, she too, would be delighted to be of service. I felt so much better. Now Dad's and my mate could come with us. My elation was short-lived. Mum had given Winkie away to a friend of hers. Irene and the kids would have taken him as a matter of course. Pluto was his mentor and mate and he'd learned to co-exist with the lively kittens. But that was how it went.

We spent the last day or two back at Mullins' hotel. Our furniture and belongings were packed and already on their way. It was heart-breaking to sit on the pub verandah after school and watch this disconsolate black and tan dog following the car we'd just sold, hoping desperately for a happy reunion with his family.

Westward Ho to Roma

Travelling south to Brisbane, it was exciting to re-visit scenes which I thought I could recognise. Better still, going in the opposite direction meant that some places that we had passed during the night on our trip north, were now able to be seen by light of day. There was little time to be spent in Brisbane – just long enough for me to become bleary-eyed thinking of Winkie - and we were soon on the Western Line heading for Roma, a bit over 500 kilometres almost due west. Apart from the undulating country in the ranges around Toowoomba where we crossed the Dividing Range, we were certainly on the western plains. Natural landmarks like mountains were very hard to find.

Leichhardt had crossed north of Roma, closer to Injune, on his audacious journeys in the mid-1840s before he mysteriously disappeared. Encouraged by the writing in his diaries, venturesome settlers followed in his tracks and in 1847, a Scot, McPherson, took up land near Roma.[11]Explorer *extraordinaire,* A.C.Gregory, selected a site for the town fifteen years later but it wasn't until 1867 that the new town was proclaimed. It took its name in honour of the wife of the Colony's first Governor. Lady Bowen also had the Diamantina River which runs into Lake Eyre named for her.

It was a prosperous town when we arrived, with Bassett's famous vineyards and winery, an important set of sheep and cattle sale-yards, a flour mill and a saw-mill and was the junction of a rail line north to Injune. Sheep and cattle grazing was the main rural industry and. with good years, provided much of the town's wealth. We soon obtained a house to rent in Arthur Street, close to the Intermediate and High School. It was an old but comfortable home by the standards of the day. We didn't yet have a refrigerator but relied on ice delivered daily for the ice chest and our bath water was heated by a chip-heater which was fed on the residue from the backyard woodheap. There were two very big bottle trees, the first I had seen at close quarters, on either side of the front gate. Arthur Street itself was, for a block or two, lined with bottle trees. A small herd

11 *New National Ausralian Encyclopedia V2* Horowitz, Cammeray. 1974

Above: Birthday in Nanango. Lennie and Donald in front. Jean, the right side of the arch.

Left: Mum and Lennie.

Below: Mum and Jean.

Above: Lennie and the bike that wouldn't travel over plague locusts.

Below Left: Dutch friend Freda and Lennie, Roma.

Below Right: Lennie, Roma.

Above: Snake charmer, Lone Pine sanctuary.

Above Right: Lennie with McWhirter Lifesaving Cup, B.G.G.S.

Right: Ruth snigging a plank with beagle hound.

Above Right: Lennie and Secret, Butcher's Hill.

Above Left: Lennie on Nurses' Quarter's steps with first dress bought with own money - 30 shillings ($3).

Below: Last day at the Boggy swimming hole. The beagles, Alan, Lennie, Joyce.

Above Right: Ruth, Boss and broken-armed Lennie.

Above Left: Ivy Vievers, Lennie and Leo, Butcher's Hill.

Below: Blue Foley (standing), Lennie and Boxer. Butcher's Hill.

Above: A radiant bride and groom, Malanda farm, December 1st 1951.

Below: Lennie on Bill's Ranger.

Above: Trooper Jack Waddell, 2nd Light Horse. Note the stylish strapped leggings.

Below: Clothing ration tickets.

Q

If this Card is found it must be returned at once to the Deputy Director of Rationing, Brisbane.

Commonwealth of Australia

1948
CLOTHING
RATION CARD

Rg. D.1

№ 80647

Issued to— Joe Fischer
Mossman

The lone casualty of the 1942 air raid on Townsville.

Townsville Daily Bulletin

of nomadic town goats loved them. They would leap agilely onto car roofs to be able to reach the leaves. This was fairly successful if the roofs were of metal but, if they were the old canvas hoods, the move could spell disaster to both goat and car-owner. The sharp hoofs penetrated the taut canvas and the goats descended onto their bellies, legs dangling, helpless – until the irate car-owner returned. Another memory of the bitumen-sealed Arthur Street was during a grasshopper plague. Their mangled bodies, squashed by the car traffic, covered the surface to quite some depth. We found that our bikes were unable to handle it. The wheels couldn't get a grip because of the pulped locusts and, no matter how we tried, our wheels would just spin. There was no traction at all and little we could do but dismount and push our bikes back home.

Jean didn't come to Roma with us. She was at University in Brisbane studying physiotherapy and boarding at the Women's College. After the first year, many of the earlier graduates had not yet found employment. Jean, more than a little disappointed, took the advice of Bob, an American G.I. with a girl friend back home and a pharmaceutical background and switched to pharmacy. She began her apprenticeship with the chemist in Roma and later rounded it off with the requisite year at the Pharmacy College in Brisbane. Being an Intermediate school which catered for the last two years of Primary school, I had to sit at the end of the year for both the Intermediate and for the more usual Scholarship. The following year, it was just a matter of moving up the corridor a few rooms, in the same building, and I was in High school.

The war was still being fought and, as Dad was keen on aeroplanes, I decided I'd be an aircraft designer. Dad encouraged this. During his stint in World War 1, he'd been 'mentioned in dispatches' and recommended for a medal but he told his Commanding Officer, thanks but he'd rather have a transfer to the Royal Flying Corps, the predecessor of the R.A.A.F. The C.O. agreed but his initial bout of malaria intervened and the war ended. Dad had a talk with the High school Principal who lived just behind us and it was agreed that I dropped Latin and took Geometric and Perspective Drawing while the boys in the Manual Training class did their more usual Trade Drawing. History was also given up and, in its place, I was to teach myself Aviation Maths on the school verandah. I didn't become an aircraft designer. I had the opportunity to further my association with horses and the war eventually ended.

Competitive Swimming Begins

Roma, with a population of about five thousand, was nearly twice as big as Tully. There were lots of boys and girls in my class and I made new friends quickly. Swimming seemed to be the favourite sport and the town had an enviable up-to-the-minute swimming pool and the best swimming coach in the

State as care-taker. Before long I joined in and was swimming in the club events, mainly in the longer distances. My mate, Denise, ended up with medals from competition in the Commonwealth Games, bringing great feelings of pride to our club and encouraging many more to take up the sport. With the usual wartime shortages, swimming togs were in short supply, however Carmel, one of our club mates, had a father who did bookie-ing at local race-meetings. To follow this occupation he often drove further to race-meetings in northern N.S.W.. This state took advantage of its Senior State status and had a much better supply of hard-to-find items. Carmel's Dad had a standing order to buy up all the lightweight Speedo swimsuits he could find. Being a team supporter and a family man, he had a fair idea of our sizes and before long we all had a Speedo swimsuit to wear for competitive events. There was a side-effect of swimming that was a little less than perfect. I still had my long plaits – the hair-dresser in Tully on a previous occasion had declined to cut them- and my hair was still a bit on the blonde side of the spectrum. The chlorine in the water turned it a definite shade of green, a little suggestive of extra-terrestrial origins. This time, with Mum's consent and a willing barber, I had my plaits cut. With short hair, I could now rinse it in the showers when I came out of the pool and my hair gradually resumed a more human appearance.

As well as swimming, we also found time for Girl Guides. Like the Junior Red Cross, the Guides were also into doing things for the servicemen and the war effort in general. I was in Magpie Patrol which Jean said was rather suitable. I don't think she liked magpies very much after the dive-bombing attacks they wreaked on us in Nanango. Our colours, worn on our pockets, were black and white. There had been Guides in Tully and I'd passed the Tenderfoot Test there in 1941 but once I joined the Roma troop I began, with the others, to study for the Second Class. We had to learn Guide Law and the Legends of the Union Jack and the Australian Flag. Signalling was taught, rudimentary semaphore and Morse Code and we learnt a few useful things like First Aid, Campfire Cookery, How to Stalk and Track and, of course, how to tie knots. My favourite was the Highwayman's Knot. It was a way to secure a horse (or whatever) that ended in a loop and a trailing end. In the case of a Highwayman, when he wanted to make a quick exit, he just had to pull the loose end, the knot unravelled and his horse, previously secured by the tricky knot, was free to gallop off with him to safety. I passed my Second Class but didn't graduate to First Class, passing only one subject in 1944, to 'Swim fifty yards and to Throw a Life-line'. By then, I had met a new and very dear friend and horses came back into my life.

My Beloved Mentor, Bessie

Through Denise, I met her Aunt Hope, who wrote beautiful poetry and knew all the station people in the district. A horselover friend of hers, Mrs. Stride, was bringing horses down from Injune for the Show and was looking for a secure spare allotment where she could hold them prior to the opening of the showgrounds. I knew just the place, not far from where we lived, with a sturdy paling fence all round and a shed with a small, lockable section at one end. Hope thought this might suit and she and I went to make the arrangements. The horses were kept there for a few days until the showgrounds were ready for them. I had gained a wonderful friend – more than that, an idol and a kind mentor. Mrs. Stride, 'Bessie', invited me out to her property, Barcoola, just out from Injune, in the brigalow. I couldn't wait. A train connected the small township with Roma and the railway was just down from our house, but it got even better. Our landlady's daughter was married to Ken who owned a large cattle property to the north of Injune. Not only would he give me a lift to Injune on his way home, he would drop me off right at Barcoola. Since meeting Bessie and her horses, I'd thought about them in every waking moment and dreamt about them at night. I wasn't disappointed.

From the time I set foot in the little house at Barcoola, I was one of the family. It was a second home. I'm afraid it showed a little and caused a few sniggers at times when I guilelessly bragged about what 'we' got for 'our' wool and the good hay 'we'd' been able to get for 'our' steers, but most people, seeing my exuberance, just smiled.

Bessie and her husband Bert (the only Cuthbert I've ever met) had no children. They devoted their lives to each other, their property and their animals. Barcoola was mainly a sheep station and bred fine-wool Merino sheep but they also fattened steers in the brigalow and, of course, there were their horses and their dogs. Bert had been in the British forces before coming to Australia after World War 1. His interest in horses, apart from good everyday riding and mustering mounts, was in jumping. Equal favourites with his horses were his dogs. He bred the black and white Border Collies and competed in sheepdog trials with continuing success. His second-in-command with the kennels was Ginger. He was, as his name suggests, a ginger dog, the colour of the famous collie, Lassie. Apparently, very occasionally in those early days of breeding, there was a throwback in colour to that side of the family. Ginger's coat, however, was short, more in line with the kelpie. Some dogs had heavy coats but most struck a happy medium of sleek coats with feathery fringes at neck and under-body. Strangely, Bert told me that his dog-buyers further west where shade was scant and temperatures very high, often asked for the heavy-coated dogs. Their thick coats acted as insulation.

Ginger understood human as well as dog language. The dogs were kept in their kennel yards when not being worked and Ginge was in charge when they were let out in the evenings. A 'go bogey' from Bert meant for Ginge to take them all to the waterhole for a cooling dip. Ginge would work them much as he'd work sheep or cattle, merely keeping a vigilant eye on them if they were doing as they were told and pouncing immediately one showed signs of rebellion. They soon learnt and dashed off happily to the swimming hole, returning just as happily once they'd cooled off. 'Go for a run' meant for Ginger to take them in the opposite direction where, in a pack, they raced around in orderly circles supervised by Ginger until he gave the signal to go home. They'd return exhilarated but in meek obedience.

One day, we were bringing in a mob of sheep and had put them through the gate into the big paddock near the yard when both Bert and Bessie left to do some more urgent chore. I was left to yard the sheep. With Ginger's help. My first feeling was of utter pride and I began to give Ginge orders in a way I thought Bert would have. Ginge totally ignored me. He went his own way, patrolling one side of the mob as it bulged out too far and generally keeping the sheep in an orderly progress to the receiving yards gates. All I could do was ride along and perform the lowliest of mustering jobs, 'bringing up the tail'. At least Ginger allowed me to shut the gate once the sheep were yarded and he even rewarded me with a slight nod of his head and a doggy smile.

Bert used to'hot'shoe his horses whereas almost everyone else around Injune shod them cold by trimming the hoof, shaping the shoe to fit and nailing it on. Perhaps it was a throw-back to his early English days. The way Bert did it, the shoe had to be shaped to fit the horse's hoof by heating it to red-hot in a forge. This is where I came in. The forge had a handle which, when turned, provided the necessary wind draught to keep the coals hot. I was the handle-turner. It was hard work but I guess the farrier's job was much, much harder. Bert had graduated from the handle-turner's job over the years to the farrier's and must have appreciated the effort needed to keep the coals hot. He insisted on paying me the princely sum of five shillings (50c) which just about covered my train fare for the next visit. The shoe was still hot when he put it against the hoof to check the fit and the smell of it is something I shall always associate with Barcoola.

Frank Dalby Davison Country

Barcoola, at 6400 acres, wasn't a large property but, with prices reasonably good, it provided a living. At one time it had been several smaller blocks, part of a W.W.1 Soldier Settlement Scheme. The weather hadn't been at all kind when the settlers arrived and the blocks proved far too small for the tough conditions. They were mostly abandoned. Combining several into the one larger block made them more successful. The writer, Frank Dalby Davison had been one of the soldier settlers and the area was the inspiration for some of his better known books and short stories. He was born in Victoria,[12] left school at twelve

12 Wilde, Hooton, Andrews.*Oxford Companion to Australian Literature* Oxford University Press Oxford. 1985

and took up work on the neighbouring farms for a couple of years before his family left for the United States. Here Frank was apprenticed into the printing trade, in which his father already had experience. He travelled over most of North America and the West Indies, writing of his experiences, but he always felt homesick for Australia and the bush. When World War1 broke out he quickly enlisted in the British Cavalry, serving in France and returning to Australia after the war in 1919. Hearing of the Soldiers Settlement Scheme and thinking that it might be the answer for him, he applied and was granted a 1280 acre block in the Injune programme. It was very tough going especially as he had a wife and two small children to support. The blocks were too small and Mother Nature conspired against the settlers by sending them, year after year, one drought to be followed by a yet more severe one. Getting nowhere except deeper in debt despite his earnest labours, he left. Four years of hard work rewarded him with nothing material but it left him with vivid memories of his life there and his memory lingers on. Local legend has it that the permanent hole that was the watering-place of the 'scrubber' band in *Mansby* was the billabong on Barcoola.

Mansby was one of the books set for study at school and I read every word several times, absorbing the atmosphere but I kept my thoughts to myself. I privately considered that the wild cattle's 'washpool' would have been closer to the foothills of the range. That didn't, however, stop me from telling the legend over and over to my fellow classmates in Roma. The billabong was the only natural, permanent water for miles and it was very, very easy to picture the scrubber mob sneaking in through the timber for a quiet drink. The hills, the Kilmoreys and Carnarvons, also attracted me strongly. With their rugged rocky cliff faces they looked like vast sheets of smoky opal when the sun shone on them at a certain angle. Pinks, misty blues and lilacs came from nowhere to display their ethereal beauty. Up in the ranges were caves with the mysterious hand stencils and other artwork of generations of Aboriginal inhabitants. I'd seen photos and had been promised a mounted escort up to see them but, though the dream survives, the reality never eventuated. I also wanted to see the rock where the Kenniffs, local poddy-dodgers and horse thiefs, burnt the bodies of their victims, Doyle and Dahlke. I'd read the account of the trial in Dad's law books at the Roma Court House although the trial did not take place there. Dad was of the opinion, doubtlessly fuelled by local lore, that 'they hanged the wrong one'. It intrigued me. What a lot it said about that clan if one was willing to sacrifice his life to save another family member. Many years later I heard of a Kenniff buried in the Charters Towers cemetery and, living then in the basalt to the north of the Towers, I made a short pilgrimage out to see it. Again the question raised its head. What happened? Who dunnit?

Harry Redford and the White Bull

Another court case that attracted me passionately was held in Roma at the Circuit Court. In fact, as a result of the questionable verdict, Roma lost the distinction of hosting the Circuit Court for many years. This was the trial of Harry Redford, said to have been the model for Rolf Boldrewood's (T.A.Browne) Captain Starlight in *Robbery Under Arms.* Redford stole the best part of a thousand head of cattle from Bowen Downs in Central Western Queensland in 1870. He successfully took them overland by a roundabout route, heading for South Australia and Adelaide where he hoped the brand would not be recognised. It was a superb feat of droving. He pioneered the route along the Barcoo River, Coopers and Strzelecki Creeks into South Australia. Stockowners, seeing the tracks of the large travelling mob, became alarmed and, checking their herds, several found that some of their cattle, too, were missing. What almost sealed his fate was a pure white Shorthorn bull that took his fancy. He could have aimed a little lower at something a little less eye-catching. The bull was truly one of a kind having been imported from Britain not long before at very considerable expense. Redford sold this bull *en route* but the new owner unwittingly took his new bargain up to the Darling Downs where it and its brand were speedily identified and Redford's game was almost up.

He was arrested, three years after the start of his epic cattle-duffing venture and put on trial at the Roma Circuit Court. The evidence against him was extensive and substantial but the verdict of the local cattlemen on the jury was 'Not Guilty'. To them it was a droving odyssey of epic proportions. No ordinary man could have accomplished it as successfully. They considered that there was no alternative but to acquit the master herdsman. The judge was not as sympathetic nor as admiring. 'Thank God, gentlemen,' he is reported to have said, 'that is your decision and not mine.' Possibly it was at his recommendation that Roma lost its Circuit Court.

When we went to Roma, the Court House was a most impressive building. The great courtroom was designed with a very high ceiling and columns above the judge's bench which supported a crest with a motto in Latin that said (don't forget I dropped Latin) 'Let justice be done even though the skies fall.' It looked most impressive but I was rather worried on the days when Dad sat there. The Court House had been built with insufficient foundations for Roma's notoriously unstable black soil. The ground must have moved slightly and a crack had appeared diagonally across one set of the impressive columns. I fervently hoped that the skies would not fall while my Dad was on the bench there.

I have been told within the last few years that the fault has been successfully remedied.

I went out to Barcoola as often as I could, by way of the convenient little train or by hitching a ride with Ken. The house at Barcoola was one of the original settlement scheme homes. It was very modest. High blocks, galvanised iron walls and roof, unlined and unceiled. There were two bedrooms on each side of a narrow hall, a front verandah with a half-wall, a back verandah closed in to accommodate a dining room and kitchen and a third side verandah with a store room at one end. The bathroom was underneath the house, corrugated iron walls, cement floor and no hot water, the 'toilet' being an outside one of the 'pit' variety.

Bessie had a cat, Flash, a beautiful tabby and white creature. Everyone had their jobs to do and Flash's was to keep snakes and mice at bay. He usually played his part well but one day Bessie was going into her bedroom to get something when she spotted a long thin snake stretched along the top of the door, with its head waving out towards her. Without a moment's hesitation, she grabbed her dressmaking scissors from where she'd been mending at the dining table. Her above-average height certainly helped. She didn't have to strain awkwardly to reach her target. One quick snip and the be-headed snake wriggled to the floor. Flash took it outside to play with. He was a strange cat in that he loved raw potato. Most carnivorous pets are strongly attracted to the smell of meat being prepared but that didn't turn Flash on like a whiff of potato did. You had only to start peeling the mealtime potato when he'd appear from nowhere, rubbing against your legs, purring and pleading in eloquent cat language for his share. Usually, the potato-peeler gave in to his entreaties and he munched happily on the small slices given to him. Cooked potato didn't have the same appeal for Flash.

Bessie's Dreams Realised - The Garryowen Trophy

Sitting around the table at the evening meal which was much more leisurely than the earlier two, Bessie would talk about her plans for her horses. She normally took a small team to Roma and often the Mitchell shows but her ambition was to go further. Her wildest dream was to be able to take a horse to Melbourne for the Garry Owen Trophy at the Royal Show. She didn't necessarily have to win it, just to have a horse good enough to enter the fabled competition. Sitting in that pokey little room, the blast of the cold westerly winds rocked the house so much on its high stumps that Bessie's collection of English china dogs and horses often toppled from their places on the narrow beams of the unlined walls. There were few that didn't show signs of fractured limbs, tails or ears that had been corrected with the never-fail adhesive of the time, Tarzan's Grip.

The Trophy was named in memory of a horse called Garry Owen, a handsome blood-bay thoroughbred who, with a two-year-old filly was lost in a stable fire at

Mentone in 1934.[13] An electric fault had started the fire and, by the time Garry Owen's distraught owner, Violet Murrell, was given the alarm by a neighbour closer to the stable building, it was already far too late. It was well into the night and Violet rushed out in her nightdress to save the horses and their minder, Billy, a blue-heeler dog. The heat of the fire was so overpowering that Violet collapsed as she tried to get the frantic animals to safety. Her husband Bill, only seconds behind her, was struck by a falling beam but managed to get his wife out, her night-clothes burning on her body. Despite all efforts, she died just thirty-seven hours after her attempted rescue. Her husband joined her just ten days later, being unable to recover from the horrific burns and the unbearable trauma he, too, had suffered. Violet's friends decided to hold the competition in their honour, naming it for Violet's beloved horse. It was a most comprehensive contest judging horse, rider and their gear. It was, at the very least, the Melbourne Cup of show-riding.

While Bessie dreamed her dreams she didn't let up on her work around the place, both inside the house and with the stock. The training of her horses filled every moment of what spare time she could engineer and they did her credit at the local shows. She was a very tall woman, 180 cms, slim and wiry. She rode one of the young horses she had been working on in the Ladies' Hack at the Mitchell Show. The horse went well and Bessie was a little disappointed when he wasn't called into the line-up from which the judge selected his final prize-winners. Always one to learn from her mistakes, Bessie wondered what they had done wrong and, after the competition, innocently asked the judge, the local Stock Inspector, where they had failed. His answer was short and to the point. The horse, a thoroughbred of just under sixteen hands high, was 'too big' for a lady's hack Bessie was relieved that they had made no errors of performance but was still not satisfied. 'What about big ladies?' she asked. His answer was a rather succinct 'Big ladies shouldn't ride.' It didn't put Bessie in her place as he may have hoped but it rather just encouraged her to try harder and the young horse won ribbons for her at later shows – and with different judges.

The war continued with increasing shortages and sacrifices though, being at school, I wasn't affected over much by them. Mum always did the best she could at home. Meat joined the rationed list in January 1944. The dearer cuts such as steak and top-quality roasts cost more ration tickets than the stewing types and offal such as liver, kidney and brains were either ration-free or rated very lowly. I used to pick up our meat after school from the old butcher shop. It still had a sign on it proclaiming it to be one of the State-owned butcher shops of much earlier days when the then Labor Government in Queensland attempted to give the people cheaper meat by means of the State taking over selected cattle stations and butcher shops. It didn't work out terribly efficiently and the scheme was

13 *The Garryowen Trophy* ed. Tim Hewat. Studmaster Press. Berwick, Victoria. 1973

abandoned. When I came back from Barcoola with Ken and not by the slower train, I usually had a present of chops or a leg of mutton roast for Mum. In return Mum would often attend to shopping for Bessie, sending the goods out by train if a willing motorist wasn't available.

Another Drought. Feeding Poddy Lambs.

The years had been rather dry and most properties, which often had two lambings per year, reduced to just one. Rearing the babies took too much from the under-nourished mothers. One year commenced with the promise of rain and a change of season so Bert and Bessie decided to work for a winter lamb crop. It was the wrong choice. After the first storms, there was no follow-up and the year turned out to be one of the driest on record. They weren't the only ones to be caught but most property-owners when faced with the then unwanted 'natural increase', hit them on the head in an attempt to save the mothers. Bert and Bessie went against the trend. I was out there when we mustered up all the ewes and lambs. The bigger lambs were put into the yards and weaned onto lucerne hay railed from Toowoomba. Unfortunately, one shipment of about three tons proved unusable. It had been wet somewhere along the line and was far too mouldy to use. Nothing could be done about it and it was discarded. The black polled steers fared better. Their numbers had been reduced and Bert followed the example of other cattlemen in the district and cut down, as required, a big bottle tree or two for them. With the trees partially barked to start them off after they'd cleaned up the nutritious foliage, the steers ate large holes right through the generous fallen trunks until there was nothing left. The 'wood' was very soft and pulpy, they liked it and it appeared to help hold their condition wonderfully well.

As it was very cold, Bert lit fires in the yards to try to provide some warmth for the lambs. For the first few days one of his reluctant early morning jobs was to throw the bodies of any overnight fatalities onto the fires. Happily, the bulk of them pulled through. The smallest lambs, about seventy of them, Bessie decided to feed on the bottle. She had a couple of milking cows which helped a little but it was in the days well before Denkavit and other calf and lamb milk-replacers had been thought up and she had to make do with what powdered milk she could scrounge. It was a rather expensive choice but it was either that or do as most of the neighbours did. Kill the lambs. When at Barcoola, I helped Bessie feed the lambs, two at a time for each of us and it took quite a long time to get through them. When I returned to town, it was my job to buy up all the powdered milk I could find, even securing Lactogen when other milk was unprocurable. The wartime shortages were still with us.

Bessie had big hands and feet as well as being so tall. She used to tell, with a smile, of how she had ordered new shoes when she was at boarding school in Toowoomba. The size that she ordered was more usual for men to wear and when the parcel arrived, in it was a pair of small children's shoes, a bit over toddler size. The shop couldn't imagine a girls' school client wanting the men's version of the shoe size. When she was feeding the lambs, her hands would get wet and the unsympathetic westerly winds blew on them causing cracks to encircle her fingers. With dust from the chaff and hay, the cracks deepened into quite serious cuts. They must have been very painful. When I came home from school, I often called in at our landlady's house if I saw her in the garden. I told her about Bessie's terribly cracked hands. She immediately went into a back room and came out with an outsize pair of soft leather gloves. They belonged to her elder son, Alf, who was a Prisoner of War in Changi. He knew Bessie, too, and she said that he would be only too happy for her to try them. I took them out on my next trip and once Bessie decided to accept them – it wasn't the done thing to rob P.O.W's of their few possessions – she put them on. Her cuts ceased to deepen and, with the gloves keeping her hands relatively dry and free of dust from the hay, they eventually healed.

The War is Over

In other ways, 1945 was a wonderful year. The Germans surrendered just after Hitler suicided in his air-raid bunker. Mussolini had already been killed by his own Italian people in protest against the war. Japan followed and surrendered after the U.S. dropped atomic bombs on Hiroshima and then Nagasaki with devastating and long-lasting effects. The Japanese signed the surrender documents aboard the U.S.S.Missouri on September 2nd.[14]

Injune, like communities all over Australia, wanted to celebrate the end of hostilities. We rode in on our horses and went through the town in a parade with our bridles be-decked with sprays of golden wattle blossom. Everyone was exuberant and optimistic about the future. Spirits were certainly high. Many of the district's young men had enlisted in the Eighth Division and it was one that suffered very badly from the taking of large numbers of prisoners after the fall of Singapore. One woman was especially jubilant. She was widowed and had lost one son in New Guinea. One, still in the Army, was alive and well but a third was in a Japanese P.O.W. camp. She was struggling to keep things going at home, her spirits kept high with the thought that two of her boys would soon be returning. We all rejoiced with her. Soon, her son in the prison camp would be home. Wonderful. He didn't make it. His health was so debilitated during his long period of captivity, that he died – just after the peace treaty was signed.

14 *Brisbane Courier Mail 2/9/1945*

The same year saw the end of my three years at the Roma schools. Mum decided I should learn the violin again so that I could take music as a subject for Junior. Jean had won a Scartwater Scholarship with her Junior pass which paid her educational expenses for the next two years. She also won a scholarship to Uni in her final year. Mum thought I should follow suit and the more subjects I took, the better. I'd passed my first violin exam at about nine years old, then jumped a year and passed the second exam, also with honours. Now the nuns were now expected to advance me four years from where I'd left off, in one brief twelve month period. It was a big ask. The practical was good. I enjoyed it but the theory section could have been Double Dutch. I disappointed my mother, again, by getting a Credit (80%) instead of Honours (85%) and didn't get a Scholarship. I passed all my school subjects including the Perspective Drawing and Aviation Maths with either As or Bs and a pretty good overall average. It wasn't good enough. My music lessons were stopped again and I was booked in at the Brisbane Girls Grammar School as a boarder for the following year. According to my mother, its teachers had the highest academic qualifications. I knew no-one going to Girls Grammar and didn't know whether to be pleased or not.

A Change of Scene – Mt. Tambourine

During the Christmas holidays I went to Mount Tambourine with a friend, Jan, another horse-crank whose parents lived there but were old Roma identities and still had a business in the town. We decided to earn a bit of pocket-money for Christmas by picking beans at a farm nearby. It was a hard, back-breaking job. Bean bushes grew a little too close to the ground. The farmer, whose sons had also seen war service, had been persuaded by them to buy some ex-army pack-donkeys. The donkeys were in the Northern Territory and all faced a death sentence if homes couldn't be found for them. Hoping that their foraging habits as related by his sons would keep in check the weedy bushes in the back paddock, he bought ten of them. He soon found that the donkeys preferred a grass diet. When that was available, feral bushes didn't interest them. He let us ride them, bareback, sitting well back toward the rump and guiding them, not with reins but with the light touch of a switchy stick applied lightly to the side of their heads. It was fun, so much so that I asked if I could buy one. I could. The farmer would take two pounds ($4) from my pay. That was the cost of getting them down from the Territory.

I couldn't wait to tell Dad of my new possession. He'd had a bit to do with pack-donkeys in the Middle East. I completely forgot in the excitement to inform Mum of the development but then I got a message from her. Get rid of it. Definitely no more donkeys wanted in the family. In the mean time, the farmer, having over-estimated the donkeys' useful appetites, didn't want to take him back. Fortunately, when Dad related my unhappy quandary to a friend from an out-of-town property, he found a willing buyer. Bob, too, had known the donkeys and the part they'd played in the Territory. He paid for my donkey and a mate and made all the necessary arrangements for them to go out to his station. I was lucky to get out of that one so easily.

Brisbane Girls Grammar School

Girls Grammar turned out to be quite an experience. I came back to Roma for holidays, at times bringing a friend with me. One was Frieda, a girl a couple of years older than her classmates. She was from the Indies, Dutch and, with her mother, sister and brother, had been placed in a camp by the Japanese when they captured those islands. Her father worked for one of the shipping companies and had been fortunate enough to be at sea and to evade capture. Dutch was her first language though her English was also very good. She did well at school and I was really impressed when she told how she coped by translating the questions into Dutch, writing her answers in that language and then re-writing them back into English for the teacher to evaluate. In the camp, their nutrition was very poor, almost to starvation point, and they all contracted beri-beri from the vitaminless diet. The symptom that carried on and was a huge embarassment to her was a rather noticeable 'pot' belly, but, eventually, with a much improved diet, her skin regained its natural colour and the pot belly disappeared. They were finally re-united with their father and did well in their new country.

For shorter holidays, I sometimes went home with one of my boarder mates who lived closer to Brisbane. I did miss my trips to Barcoola but one holidays coincided with the Roma Show. It was a special one, the anniversary of some special event. Bessie told me that I could ride my favourite mount, Thunder, and that she had nominated me in a rider event. This was not the Best Lady Rider that most shows held but was Roma's upper-class equivalent, Most Graceful Lady Rider. I felt very proud if not all that confident but I felt that Bessie must have thought I could manage it. Now being sixteen years old, I was considered to be a lady by the Show Society.

A Doubtful Show Ribbon

All went well until I was instructed to slow-canter Thunder out from the line-up to the outer edge of the ring, halt, then turn and trot back to the judge. It would have been simple except that just as I began to gather my reins to 'halt' Thunder, the Catherine Wheel, stationary and very silent until then, decided to start up with a flurry of activity and noisiness. It was only metres from us, just outside the ring. Terror-stricken, the country-bred Thunder ducked his head and put in a couple of protest pig-jumps before I could get his head up, regain control and trot him, sedately I hoped, at a rising trot, to the waiting judge. The onlookers loved it but the only person more surprised than me when the steward put the red (second prize) rosette on my arm, was Bessie. She couldn't believe it. It went against all the rules. Then one of her friends remarked that at least I didn't fall off. I kept my seat in the saddle and you couldn't get anything more graceful than that. I don't think Bessie agreed and it was best not to bring up the subject of Lady's Riding events for some time. Dad was sorry he'd missed it. The rough-riding bit appealed to him and he was pleased I didn't disgrace him by falling off, but the thought of me as a 'graceful lady' he found rather humourous.

At B.G.G.S. there were very few boarders, about forty, in a school of five hundred or more pupils. We were rather unimportant and had little standing until the second year that I was there and a new boarder arrived from Monto, Daphne. She wasn't even hoping to go on to University as most of the girls did but was studying in the commercial class. The year before, our very popular head girl and captain of the successful tennis team, had failed to gain a University scholarship and decided to repeat the year and try again. Margaret was very popular and a great all-rounder at sport so it was little short of astounding when the new boarder from Monto took the crown from the reigning champ in the college's own tennis championships. We boarders were beside ourselves with pride. Daphne's wonderful success took us all up several rungs in the ladder of social status. We were almost equals. Daphne continued on her winning run proving her talent not only in the inter-school competition but continuing on to win both nationally and internationally. It certainly gave the Boarders a boost.

Walking The Dog

The subjects that I took were Science orientated, both Maths, Physics and Zoology. Most of my classmates were very clever scholars and nearly all hoped to go on to University. Many did, becoming doctors, scientists and even one engineer, some obtaining positions overseas. Our headmistress 'Bloss', short for Blossom, Lilley was a descendant of a very well-known and rather eccentric family. Miss Lilley had more than her share of both the fame and the eccentricity. She said she much preferred 'the Arts' but the classes over which she presided as English Mistress were the B or Science forms. Maybe she hoped to civilise the savages. She had a faithful little Yorkshire terrier, Geordie, who used to accompany her everywhere about the school. As Bloss was quick to find fault and quicker still to inform the perpetrator of her wrath, we held Geordie in exceedingly high regard. He trotted into the class-room a good two minutes before his mistress arrived. This endearing habit gave us time to stop talking, tidy our desks, get out our English books ready and to stand to attention submissively as Miss Lilley entered. It was the Senior boarders responsibility to take Geordie for Sunday walks. Two girls performed the escort duty. Dressed in our white 'church' frocks, with black lisle stockings and our school hats, we caused some interest as we walked along the path bordering the Park. The grass growing along the sides of the concrete path was usually long enough to obscure the sight of little woolly Geordie so that passers-by in their cars would stare at the sight of these two oddly-dressed girls walking along with a taut lead angled to the ground ahead of them. There was still an Army camp nearby and soldiers found us a great source of amusement. We rarely accomplished our trip without loud and rather saucy comment. Still, it was a chance to get out of the school grounds, Geordie was a sweetie and escort duty was considered an honour. We were all devastated when Geordie suddenly died. I guess Miss Lilley felt it even more. The Boarders had a whip-around and raised a small amount which our dormitory mistress took to Miss Lilley with the thought of buying her another canine pet. She was quite overwhelmed at our offer but we suspected that she gave the donation to the Salvos, a favourite charity of hers. She did buy another dog. It lacked Geordie's self-reliance. Bloss entered the class-room unannounced with the new dog following demurely at her heels.

Before we were about to sit for our Senior, the University matriculation examination, Miss Lilley spent one of her tuition periods discussing what we hoped to do for our future. Most of the girls intended to, and did, go on to university. I was of two minds. I still had visions of horses and mustering but realised that was more than a little out of place at somewhere as illustrious as B.G.G.S. I'd be a vet. and look after other people's animals. When it came to my turn, I stood up, confident that my reply would meet with Miss Lilley's approval, and said, 'I want to be a veterinary surgeon, Miss.' Her reaction was totally unexpected and rather off-putting. After telling how big, brawny, crass male students would just elbow me aside, she gave her opinion, 'Get a job in a newspaper office, even if it is only sticking stamps on envelopes.' I wasn't convinced.

My First Acceptance and Cheque

However, I had, in a very small way already embarked on a journalistic career. Girls Grammar wasn't over-endowed with record-breaking swimmers in its team and, with my Roma experience, I was accepted. I was also a bit of a nuisance. No one could remember having a boarder in the team previously and there were no arrangements for one to undertake training. The team trained together several times a week at the Valley Baths, quite some distance from the school. Finally, I was instructed to breakfast early in the kitchen by myself, walk down to the city and catch the tram at Edward Street for the Valley. After the training session I'd be able to return to the school with the rest of the team. It worked out well except for a minor financial hitch. Mum had again forgotten to send my pocket-money for the term, two shillings or twenty cents each week that was to provide soap and toiletries, school pads and pencils and now an unexpected daily tram fare.

I got to be quite good mates with one in particular of the kitchen staff. I already knew their value as a liaison with the outside world. Kathleen suggested, after I'd told her over porridge and toast of my bush-orientated stories and dreams, that I write a short story – with a romantic interest - for the Brisbane *Telegraph.* She showed me a couple of the stories that had been printed and I decided to try. It was '*Dear Diary*' in a simulated diary form telling of a bush governess's crush on the station-owner's handsome son. It ended with a rather trite entry, 'He's asked me to marry him.' Together we selected a suitable pen-name and Kathleen made all the necessary arrangements to have it typed by one of the day-girls and sent to the *Telegraph.* Imagine how I felt one morning when she handed me a letter, addressed to her, asking would she accept three guineas for its publication! We couldn't get the answer back quickly enough. Kathleen refused to take any payment as my 'literary agent' and the three guineas (six dollars 30cents) was mine. That amounted to thirty-one and a half week's pocket money! A fortune. My financial worries were over. Needless to say, it was a one-off success, but it couldn't have come at a better time.

Before my windfall I was caught without pocket-money on a trip to Lone Pine Sanctuary. One mistress, Miss Weaver, used to take us on interesting excursions when she was on boarding duty. She loved musicals and when one came to town she took us all to the matinee. Roses were also a love of hers and a visit to the Kangaroo Point Gardens was a must when the roses came into bloom in the spring. Lone Pine's koalas were another of her favourites. I had enough money to get in through the gate but when the girls lined up to have their photos taken with the cuddly marsupials for two shillings and six pence (25c) I had to think of a good excuse. Not dreaming that the attendant would open the snake cage for one girl, I said in what I hoped was an offhand tone, 'No thanks. I'd rather have mine taken with the snakes.' No sooner had I said my piece but he'd opened the cage and draped a horribly big squirmy snake over my shoulders. The other girls thought it was hilarious and I had no problem at all in borrowing the photographic fee. Some also ordered their own copies.

Our swimming went well. I scored ribbons in the backstroke and one of the longer races and our team won the glamour event, the McWhirter Lifesaving Cup. The success entitled me to have the swimming team's name and date added to the pocket of my school blazer.

A Day at the Ekka

Miss Lilley was always keen for us to visit the Brisbane Exhibition on People's Day. We were sternly lectured beforehand on what was acceptable behaviour and what was definitely not. Understandably, we all had to stay in groups, usually with a teacher in control. Fairy floss and other goodies were to be taken only in moderation and, on returning to our dormitories, we were to have very thorough hot showers, wash our hair and, as a second crowning glory, gargle with a salty mixture provided by Matron from Sick Bay. If we did all this, we would come to no harm, no abductions, no tummy upsets and no Showground germs to infect the rest of the school. It was a light enough price to pay. Naturally, some of us horsey, country girls persuaded the mistress to let us visit the horse stalls. Here I met up with Bessie and her new horse, Royal Marine. When the drought broke, the price of wool soared to a sky-high 'a pound a pound'. Bert managed to keep the wool from the little pet lambs apart from the others, baled it separately and once sold, presented Bessie with the cheque. She was to do whatever she wished with it. The rest would easily pay the property's running costs and for the past drought-feeding program. Bert knew well what Bessie's wish would be. She bought a young but not-fast-enough thoroughbred racehorse. He received his name, Royal Marine, as a tribute to Bert's earlier war service but his name also brought him into contact with two young Royal Marines who were on leave. Being horse-lovers, they, too, came to the Exhibition to observe the skills of horses and riders. They were quite impressed with Royal Marine's performance. He won two blue, first prize, ribbons. Bessie's dream, at long last, had started to come true. Characteristically generous, and associating the young men with her good fortune, she insisted on presenting them with the ribbons. Her very first Royal Show ribbons.

Royal Marine did well and had many admirers but he wasn't quite what Bessie had in mind. She had offers to buy him and finally let him go to a good horsewoman and a good home. By this, she had set her sights on another thoroughbred, a horse that was racing in Brisbane but which also competed on the same Western Circuit that Bessie covered with her show team. It was love at first sight and she didn't want to lose the chance of getting this particular horse. She asked veteran horse-dealer, Athol Strong, to try to secure the offer for her. Bessie had to wait, not very patiently she admitted, for almost twelve months before, in early 1950, he came on the market. She immediately bought him at what she said was the 'ridiculously high price of four hundred pounds', today's eight hundred dollars. He still had racing on his mind and it took many long hours of lungeing him on a lead and many more miles of long, settling rides culminating in a short course of stockwork before she had him going well enough to enter him in the Brisbane Royal that year. Her hunch and her hard work paid off. And the results nearly exceeded her dreams. Not only did Gallant win his hack classes but Bessie won the broad purple sash of Champion Lady Rider and Bert the Gentleman Rider Turnout on him as well. The following year, 1951, he did even better, winning for her the coveted Champion Hack. Bessie had hoped to take him from there on to Melbourne to realise her dream and to enter him in the Garry Owen. He had shown that he would not let her down but the seasons were against her. There was another drought and work had to come before idle pleasure. They returned home immediately after Brisbane.

Even worse was to follow next year. Everything was going according to plan. Bessie had Gallant working well and Bert had a very good young horsewoman to help train and ride his show-jumper. The week before the Brisbane Show, Bert and Bessie were watching Bert's horse being ridden over the jumps on the training oval they'd set aside down near the yards, when Bert suddenly suffered an unexpected heart attack and fell down – dead. That put a heart-rending end to that year's show plans.

Bessie's Dream Realised

A lesser person might have given up the dream but, with everyone encouraging her, Bessie took Gallant on down to the Sydney Royal in 1953. He did more than well. Six blue ribbons, the Champion Hack and the coveted Colonel A.V. Pope Cup. Bessie, too, and most deservedly, won a sash for the most successful exhibitor in the Saddle Horse events. Buoyed-up and with her dream rejuvenated, she flew herself and Gallant to the Adelaide Show. Contrary to some of the warnings Bessie was given, Gallant wasn't at all upset during his plane ride and she reported on landing that he'd even eaten 'a bucket of feed' on the flight. At Adelaide, he took out the Champion Hack thus removing any trace of doubt that he wasn't of a high enough standard for the Garry Owen. In this event he did more than just strut his stuff without disgraceful incident, he came third.

The following year, the happy pair returned again to Sydney and actually improved on the previous year's glowing results. Bessie was ecstatic. It seemed a long way from the Barcoola dining-room dreams with the china horses and dogs toppling from their resting places and the winds whistling icily through the cracks. Adelaide again rewarded them with the Champion Hack and then it was Melbourne's turn. Gallant was on a roll. He did his very best in the Garry Owen, giving a performance that even his critical owner found hard to fault. Even so, she was unprepared when the steward called out the number of the winner of the event – number 43. Gallant's identification. They had won! As Bessie stepped Gallant up to receive his sash, she said 'pride gave way to tears of joy'.

It is a wonderful story when you think of what seemed a most impossible dream, a goal Bessie kept before her even when personal tragedy and the seasons intervened. It seemed almost unattainable in that little galvanised iron cottage at Barcoola but hard work, dedication and a good choice of horse more than paid off. The impossible dream was realised and Bessie was sure Bert was there in spirit to encourage her along the way. Tragically, there was a very sad postscript just a year later at the Sydney Royal. Bessie was exercising Gallant in Centennial Park when he was hit by a car. His injuries were such that there was no alternative but to put him down. Bessie was left with her impossible dream fulfilled but with also with a cruelly 'broken heart and loneliness'. She was a wonderful woman, an inspiration to me and to many, many others.

Back North to Cooktown

By the time I sat for my Senior examination at B.G.G.S., Mum and Dad had moved again. They returned to Cooktown but this time Dad would be the Clerk of Petty Sessions cum Warden and not just the Clerk's clerk. The last term at B.G.G.S. had been rather exciting. Our Physics mistress, 'Tuff', had a brilliant scientific mind. She and her husband had both worked for the police Department in Forensics. Tuff couldn't understand how we found it impossible to grasp scientific intricacies immediately. I'm sure we caused her many sleepless nights as the examinations loomed closer. Finally, she came into the lab one morning with a smile on her face and waved a sheet of paper at us. As soon as we were seated she explained the plan. She and her husband had gone through all the Physics papers set for the last fifteen years and the list on her waved page was what they thought would be the most likely questions to be given us. It wasn't long before we had the subjects on her list almost word perfect and her choice proved to be spot-on. With the benefit of an occasional alternative question we were well-grounded on the subjects set. To Tuff's immense relief, none of us failed and most obtained very good results.

Goodbye To Boarding School

Another happy occasion at year's end was the school concert organised by the boarders. Our dormitory rather excelled with a rendition of the old folksong, *Frankie and Johnnie.* Our best pianist played the accompaniment and, dressed in my jodhpurs, shirt, cowboy hat and boots plus a very big silver-paper star, I was the Sheriff and sang the words telling the story. Everyone loved it but the applause was the loudest and most spirited when Frankie took her John to the graveyard. 'He' was laid out on a short, borrowed laundry trolley which almost got away from poor Frankie, dressed, seductively we hoped, in a draped cubicle curtain, and began to topple over the steps leading up to the stage. Johnnie quickly came back to life and the audience heartily responded.

We also had a farewell school ball with the day-girls in the Assembly Hall. Bloss wasn't too enthused about our choice of partners for the occasion and gave us her opinion of the Boys Grammar boys as 'inky-fingered schoolboys in short pants'. We had to go further afield and most of us borrowed acquiescent older cousins or the surplus cousins of friends, to help out. The mother of my mate Gwen, had a male dressmaker in Brisbane who made her special occasion frocks. She took us shopping to buy material, took our measurements and requirements and left the rest to him. We didn't have to wear white and my choice was a bright floral taffeta with a long white satin petticoat. The neckline, by no means plunging but very wide, extended to the tips of my shoulders and was accentuated by a frill. Perfectly legal. The days of Victory Clothing were over. When we went to try our frocks on and pick them up from the dressmaker under the chaperonage of Gwen's mother, the dressmaker had also made me a silver brocade short-sleeved bolero from a piece of left-over material he had found. On the night, Bloss made her usual and not unexpected comments but the music was great and we had a marvellous night.

A day-girl friend learnt the violin and practised at school each weekday. She offered to lend me her fiddle as she considered that I shouldn't waste the years I had put in to learning to play. We selected a Hungarian dance from her repertoire, with crashing chords and fancy fingering. By the time the term ended I was eagerly looking forward to surprising Dad with it when I arrived home.

Cooktown at Last

The trip to Cooktown was even better than I'd hoped for. Jean and Theresa came, too. Once we reached Cairns by train, we caught the little mail launch that the Hayles family operated each week between Cairns and Cooktown. Dad was at the wharf to meet us and there were others in the background keen to see what the Warden's daughters looked like. Cooktown, like the rest of the Peninsula, was rather short of girls. I didn't hear the verdict on Theresa, who would more than have held her own on both counts but I was later told of the decision concerning Jean and me. 'One's not a bad sort but the other's 'ighly intelligent'. We never worked out which was which but my meeting with one of Dad's mates, the little girl next-door, didn't go well. She burst into tears at the sight of me and ran back into her own house. Dad had told her his 'baby' was coming up on the boat and she'd expected someone a little younger, about her age, two or three years, to play with.

When we unpacked and settled in I asked Mum where was my violin. I couldn't wait to play for Dad. It was on the top of the wardrobe in our room. The 'wardrobe' was of a popular type for those days. A corner shelf was made at above head-height with a curtained front hiding a rail for coathangers. Quickly

I got the case down, so eager to tune up and play my piece for Dad but found to my heartbreak and horror that it had been under what was probably the only leak in the roof. The violin was in pieces. The glue had given away entirely to the moisture. I threw myself on the bed and cried.

Later, when Mum asked what to do with it, I had in no way recovered and in a sulky voice said, 'You may as well stick it in the copper fire'. When I went out to Butcher's Hill a few weeks later, Ruth's mother, an excellent pianist, told me of an old boat-builder in Cooktown who made guitars and other stringed musical instruments. He'd certainly be able to fix it. I told her about Sydney May and his violin experts and she agreed that maybe I should try them first. They'd know what could be done. I could hardly wait to tell Dad that all was not lost. As soon as I arrived back home I asked Mum for the violin which was no longer in its doubtful resting place. 'You told me to burn it.' She'd done just that. It was probably the first time Mum had ever taken notice of anything I had said.

Jean and Theresa could only stay for a couple of weeks and we certainly made the best of them. Dad took us to the North Shore in his outboard. We swam, beach-combed for shells on the nearby beaches and climbed every available hill. As it was the Christmas season, there were fund-raising balls. One just before Christmas and one, naturally, to see the New Year in. My new long frock came in handy. I wore the dress itself to the first ball and the satin petticoat with the silver bolero to the other without anyone except the family waking up to the subterfuge. We all had a marvellous time even when we sneaked outside to watch the boys roll an empty tank down the street towards the harbour. It ended up almost inside the Post Office so we all rushed inside and pretended we'd never left the hall all night, too busy dancing. It was the perfect time to arrive in Cooktown. Everyone was there for the Balls and I met so many friends. That is where I met my friends Joyce and Ruth who had come in from Butcher's Hill station for the festivities. Ruth was my age, Joyce the same age as Jean and training to be a nurse. Butcher's Hill was a well-known cattle station, a day's ride from Helenvale which was able to be reached by vehicle. They invited me out to visit. Ruth may even have been a bigger horse-crank than I was. They had to return home straight after the New Year's Ball but I promised them I'd accept their invitation and go out to see them as soon as possible. Norman, from Helenvale, was the mailman and could deliver me there with the mail.

The Tragedy of the Watsons of Lizard Island

Jean and Theresa duly returned south so I was left to my own devices. Finding something to do was easy. I just went to the Court House and 'helped' Dad with the stock returns that every stockowner in the State was obliged to fill in and send to the Court House each year. Statistics were gathered from them but when I became more intimately involved with filling them in, I appreciated the meaning of the words, 'lies, rumours and statistics'. There were no interesting cattle-duffing cases to read up. Nothing at all in the class of Harry Redford but there were others like the tragic story of the ill-fated Mrs. Watson and her baby, Ferrier. Coincidentally, Bessie's maiden name was Ferrier, so it made me feel even closer to the unfortunate pair. Mary Watson, whose body with its bony fingers clutching her baby son's tiny hand, was found the day before what should have been her twenty-second birthday, 16th January 1882,[15] was Cooktown's earliest heroine. Emigrating from Cornwall with her family, she travelled north to Cooktown to take a position advertised in Brisbane's *Courier* by a Monsieur Bouel for 'a suitable governess for two children'. The situation turned out to be not quite as advertised – or expected – but Mary met and quickly fell in love with a man much older than herself, Captain Robert or Bob Watson. He was besotted with her and she saw in him many of the traits she had so admired in her beloved father. They married at the church in Furneaux Street on 30th May 1880.

Watson and his partner Percy Fuller had boats and were engaged in the profitable *beche de mer* industry. These sea-slugs or sea cucumbers (they had a greenish hue) were supposedly both a stimulant and an aphrodisiac as well as a succulent food delicacy much in demand by the wealthier Chinese. The men had set up a base at Lizard Island, north-east of Cape Flattery where Mary joined them. She had at least one 'holiday' in Cooktown. On 3rd June 1881, their son Ferrier was born. As Mary, an avid diarist, recorded 'no doctor required.' She and the mid-wife Mrs. Boland managed the birth satisfactorily themselves. With the new baby, Mary returned to Lizard Island. *Beche de mer* catches were decreasing so Watson and Fuller planned to shift their operational base further north to Night Island. Mary asked if she and baby Ferrier, now three months old, could remain at Lizard while they made an inspection of the new outpost. Not seeing any pressing problems, Watson agreed. The men hoped to return within six to eight weeks and the family would be comfortably settled in their new home on Night Island for Christmas.

Mary missed Bob's company but with the baby and her household chores and diary-keeping, there was plenty to occupy her time. She even tried to make a pet of one of the resident lizards. Watson left two trusted Chinese, Ah Leong and Ah Sam, on Lizard to assist Mary and to supervise the preparation of some *beche de mer.* No one could have predicted the tragedy that developed from there. Aboriginals, resenting the intrusion on their island and knowing that the two white men had sailed off, fatally speared Ah Leong in the island's vegetable plot and menacingly surrounded the little cottage. Ah Sam was also speared, but not fatally, as he ventured out to secure some water. There was no way Mary could

15 Jillian Robertson *Lizard Island* Hutchinson, Australia. n.d.

summon help. She would have to go looking for assistance. Her only means of escape was the metal ship's tank in which their remains were found by the crew of the *Kate Kearney* on Howick No. 5 Island. With great difficulty Mary and the wounded Ah Sam put what supplies they could into the tank and manoeuvred it across the beach to the water. Everything went against them. Although Mary hoisted up one of Ferrier's shawls as a distress flag it failed to attract the attention of a passing vessel. When they were able to make a landing, it was on a waterless islet. Ferrier, Mary and Ah Sam perished from thirst. Ironically, when their bodies were located, rain had fallen and the tank containing Mary and her baby also held rain water.

Understandably, Robert Watson was distraught as was the whole of Cooktown's population. The minister who had married Robert and Mary just twenty months earlier performed the funeral service to a crowd of hundreds of townsfolk and bushmen. In 1886, with funds readily subscribed by the residents, the memorial to the 'heroine of Lizard Island' was erected at the wharf end of Cooktown's main street.

I was familiar with the story and looked up the relevant death certificate in the Court House records. The cause of death was 'Thirst' but someone had pencilled in the margin 'lack of water'. I thought that rather strange until, quite a few pages further on in the Death Register, I came across the Death Certificate of the Coroner who had signed the certificates for Mary, Ferrier and Ah Sam. He had died of 'Delirium Tremens'. Apparently there are differing kinds of thirsts.

Another entry that interested me was for a young Aboriginal, Peter Wallace who died and was buried at Butcher's Hill. Here the undertaker's name was given as Doreen M. Wallace, my mate Ruth's mother. Peter was one of three Aboriginal children she had fostered at their mother's request. Peter contracted what was later thought to be rheumatic fever and, despite Mrs. Wallace's care, died. As the men were camped out mustering, Doreen and her loyal Aboriginal helper, Charlie Wallace, carried out the burial. Peter was buried wrapped in his swag and with his hat, boots and whip.

On a brighter note was the marriage registration of Dad's clerk George Comino who married one of the town's very popular nurses. All the names on the certificate were the genuine signatures of the participants, not just a run-of-the-mill entry by the Registrar.

Abandoned Treasure

Behind the Court House was a spare allotment with a closed-in shed that became one of my haunts. It also had a beautiful well with the water level so high you could scoop the sweet water up in a pannikin. I overheard Dad telling someone that the block was for sale. The price of under a hundred pounds

($200) was relatively miniscule and I wracked my brains trying to find out how I could buy it and set it up as horse stables. The inside of the little building housed a treasure trove, old 'military' saddles and lesser saddlery items, a pile of corroding horseshoes and tea cases. These were cubic shaped plywood boxes of a bit less than a metre square, originally used for the tea purchased by the grocery shops. The tea cases housed reams and reams of old yellowing papers. I intended to investigate them more closely but a pair of strange leather leggings caught my eye.

Dad had young friends, in their late teens or early twenties, who had horses in Cooktown. Many of them were in from tin mines at Rossville or from the cattle camps on surrounding properties. It would be no trouble at for them to select from their store of horses a good, quiet, reliable mount for me. Alan Burn's buckskin, Creamy, was my selection of those offered. Creamy came complete with saddle and bridle and Dad kindly provided a saddlebag and quartpot to round off my outfit. To accompany my horsey friends on their rides there was a code of behaviour to which I readily acquisesced. I was to ask no stupid questions and, unless I had something of value to import, speak only when spoken to. I was to 'keep up' and not cause my mates to lessen speed when chasing brumbies and make sure Creamy neither wiped me off on a tree nor fell down a hidden hole with me. Above all, I wasn't to get lost. As time went by, I could accomplish most of these conditions and my riding ability increased considerably.

The old military saddles in the shed had little appeal. I'd seen saddles something like them used by soldiers in World War 2. They were very simple in design. More like a light packsaddle with a slightly raised pommel in front and a low cantle at the back than the ringer's favourite genuine Weineke stock saddle. The leggings were a different matter. My horsemen mates all wore leggings. There were simple 'pull-ons' like the tops of tall riding boots, which were slipped over the foot before the elastic-sided boot was put on. Some had a thin greenhide lace that passed under the boot in front of the heel from the bottom of the legging. This was to keep them anchored in position but they weren't really necessary. 'Springside' leggings with a nifty vertical side fastening could be put on after the boots and 'Concertina' leggings with flexible corrugations around the leg were the pinnacle of fashion.

I gathered up these strange leggings, very dry from lack of care and use, and took them to the office to show Dad. They worked on a wrap-around system being shaped to fit the contour of the calf and were secured by two straps which encircled them and, buckled up, kept the legging in place. They were something like the ones of old Light Horse days Dad said and they were badly in need of a dose of neatsfoot oil to soften them. If I thought they'd be any use to me I could try them. Georgie Comino thought them a bit of an antiquated joke but I couldn't wait to try them out the next time I went for a ride with my mates.

Jeans hadn't come into use in North Queensland in those days. I wore jodhpurs so did Alan and, at times, some of the others but the men usually wore moleskins or 'stockman's cut' trousers. These had slender, tapered legs with reinforcing panels where each leg gripped the saddle. They were made of a lightweight but strong material called Venetian Twist but I don't know if the gondoliers also wore them. Long sleeved shirts, with the sleeves rolled up, an Akubra hat and a leather belt, strong enough to be used to tie down a cleanskin mickey (bull) when thrown by the ringer, completed the outfit. The leather belt was adorned with matching pouches to hold a pocketknife, watch, matches and sometimes a snakebite outfit of lancet and Condy's crystals. I had the leather belt but envied my mates their useful pouches. Dad gave me a smaller, more feminine, version of a pocketknife and I carried it in my trouser pocket.

Riding With the Boys

The Christmas-New Year period was the time my new friends took a break from work. It was usually too wet for mining and most cattle stations allowed for a break about this time, too. There were very few girls of my age in Cooktown at the time and the ones that I had met at the balls had jobs in town so that I was the only girl in the horsey crowd. I had a marvellous time. There was somewhere to go nearly every day. A favourite ride was to go to Walker's Bay to run brumbies. I wasn't much use but I managed not to get in the way and not impede the capture of the wild horses. At Walker's Bay we had a change from tea when the billy was boiled. The water there, from a soaky spring, was brackish, a bit salty, so we drank coffee instead.

Once the horses were yarded and safely broken-in, I think I might have been of some little use. When the horse was educated enough to be ridden outside the yards, I provided escort duty. The young horses behaved much better in the company of another horse. Things usually went well unless we ran into Monty Williams' goats. They had the run of the town and the old billygoat seemed to think he was of more importance than the local mayor. If he saw a colt out for an educational walk that was reacting to his threatening presence, he really laid it on. He'd rear up to his full height, pirouette on his hind toes and advance towards the frightened horse in a menacing way. The horse-breakers did not like old Monty's billygoat. I did blot my copy-book one day but fortunately no harm was done. March (or is it Marsh?) flies were very prolific. They landed on both horse and rider in hordes. We rode with sleeves rolled down to the wrist but that didn't deter them. Riding alongside Royce, his young horse's rump was completely covered with the winged marauders. I was so close, I couldn't resist and unthinkingly made a swipe at them. The horse objected to my provocative action and tried to put in a couple of little pig-jumps. Luckily, Royce had his mount well under control. Not only was he an excellent horseman, but gentlemanlike, he never uttered one word of reproof. He didn't need to. My shame and humiliation were instant and infinite. I'd also learnt a lasting lesson. Think before you act.

My mother didn't altogether approve of me riding out with the boys. She had no need to worry, as Dad well knew. I was in extremely good hands. While accepted as a mate, I was treated as a lady. No swear word was ever uttered in my hearing and I couldn't have asked for more considerate guardians. Faced with their very much superior riding skills, I was more than ever cognisant of my shortcomings but they did all they could to booster my confidence. Royce had a magnificent black horse I would have given anything to ride. He was a horse to dream about, high-spirited and a beautiful mover but I realised my limitations and didn't ask. It would have been difficult for Royce to refuse my request. The faithful Creamy suited me well.

Alan and John

Alan worked a tin mine at times, helped out in mustering and droving camps sometimes as a cook and even, at times, took the cook's job on at one of the pubs or the local hospital. As a child he'd contracted polio and was fortunate to recover as well as he did. He walked with a pronounced limp, dragging one leg a little but that didn't stop him doing just whatever needed to be done. Alan had a mate, John Barry, whom I met later and whose friendship I treasured over many years. They both had these bad limps and were apt to refer to each other as 'that hoppy-legged bugger'. Both also had lovely singing voices when they could be prevailed upon to use them. John's misfortunes began when returning from a race meeting in Coen during World War 2. He and his mate, Ian, decided to go down to Cooktown and there to enlist in the Army. They didn't get that far. Seeing a dingo menacing a group of cows with baby calves, they took off after the predator. John was right up, almost on it and ready to strike it down, when his horse stumbled. The fall broke John's neck. The doctor's prognosis was that John would never walk again but John had other ideas.

At that time, there was, on the Atherton Tableland, a genius of a man named Kjelberg He specialised in rehabilitating people whom other doctors had given up on. It took several years but the man who was told that he'd never walk again, walked away from Kjelberg's clinic with a joyful smile, ready to take on anything that life offered. John was never one to trade on his disability. If anything, he did his utmost to show that he suffered from no disability. If cleanskin cattle were sighted in a muster, John was usually the one who galloped first to the lead. This often had disastrous results as considerations for his own safety rarely entered John's head. He broke almost a record number of limbs and minor bones over his years in the cattle camps. He also liked his rum when time and opportunity permitted and, as a result of imbibing too keenly, lost one of his kidneys to the surgeon's knife. None of these setbacks appeared to hold him back at all. He lived life to the full.

At one time John was our cook while I was helping my husband bring a big mob of cattle from Coen to Mareeba. It was a dry start to the year and our horses were getting weaker each day. Going through Musgrave, John's sister Mary Shephard's property, John spotted a Musgrave horse he had previously ridden and decided to 'borrow' it for the trip. His decision proved rather disastrous. The horse, with the Peninsula's usual loathing for 'horse thieves', bucked and threw John onto the base of the hardest of all timber, an ironwood tree. He struck the lower part of its trunk with the upper part of his own. The cattle continued on their way as Hank Morris miraculously appeared from Dixie on his way to pick up loading at Musgrave in his trusty Fergie tractor and trailer. He'd take John in with him. John's sister, Mary, in charge of the Telegraph Station at Musgrave, could contact the Aerial Ambulance in Cairns for assistance and John would be on his way, set for yet another recovery.

Before Hank arrived on the scene, John asked me to examine his back. Admittedly it looked as if the shoulder that made first contact with the tree was damaged but John tried to guide me more explicitly in the diagnosis. "Just look at me back. Both sides should look the same. If it don't, that's where the trouble is." It was hard to find the 'trouble' by John's method. He had broken so many ribs and other bones that, with the big incision from the missing kidney adding to the confusion, neither side of his back seemed to match the other at all.

Hank got him safely (if not comfortably) to Musgrave and he was flown to Cairns Base Hospital with a few hours. With John's record, he soon recovered from his broken shoulder and took up station work again. He was a very good self-taught saddler and often acted as travelling saddler visiting stations, counterlining saddles, making new and mending old, gear. He came to us at Crocodile in the 1960s to get our gear in order. Our second son, Billy, not yet doing Correspondence School lessons, became John's mate. He followed John everywhere, dragging one little leg just as his hero did and was content to spend hours with John, passing him what he needed for the job in hand. John was anxious to get up to Maitland Downs to do up their saddlery gear. He'd been expected up there for some time and was feeling rather guilty but, if the truth be known, the effect of all his old injuries had just about caught up with him. His ability to do all the things he hoped to accomplish was lessening but I didn't realise what John was getting at when he and I were sharing a pot of tea for smoko one afternoon and discussing his injuries. "Oh," said John, "I'll be buggared if the old devil'll catch me in a corner. I'll go when I'm good and ready."

John's Farewell

It was explained all too sorrowfully when John finally finished his work at Maitland Downs and moved back to Laura. John and his mates were all drinking companionably at the bar until closing time when they retired to their rooms. George Watkin, the proprietor, went to the engine room to turn off the lighting plant motor. No one was prepared for what happened next. A loud report from a gun. John had shot himself. He'd gone when he was 'good and ready'.

While my days were mostly spent in company with my ringer mates, there were other things to do. For a start, although Mum had Laura, the tracker's wife, to help with the weekly washing, I was the one to whom other domestic chores fell. I was chief washer-upper, kerosene fridge-filler, silver polisher and curator of the furniture which had to be dusted and O'Cedar polished each Saturday morning without fail. Through both Mum and Dad I got to know an old Cooktown identity, Gladys Black. Gladys's father had opened one of the first stores in Cooktown and Gladys, never marrying, had carried it on. A Chinese family operated a store closer to the wharf while Herb and Kath Savage did a brisk trade at their general store in Charlotte Street across the corner from the Commercial (now the Cooktown) Hotel. This led would-be disparagers of the once-thriving goldrush town to comment that the only stores there were operated by 'Chinese, Blacks and Savages'.

When I met Miss Black she was making decorative pincushions and needed filling for them. I was to collect cotton for her from the bushes that grew wild behind the old Post Master's residence, almost adjoining my magic stableyard. It was a pleasure to harvest the cotton bolls for Miss Black and I soon had a bag of them, seedless and all teased out, for her. In return I was treated to a glass of home-made lemon syrup, a piece of cake and the story of how the cotton came to be growing there.

James Dick - Visionary

The hero of the story was a remarkable man called James Dick. He was one of the first prospectors but was also a businessman with a general store in town and a farming property, Excelsior, on the other side of the harbour, near Boiling Springs, north of Flaggy Siding on the Cooktown to Laura rail line. Apart from many other good qualities, James Dick was a visionary, but one with a very practical background. His faith in the ability of the land around Cooktown to produce just about anything the markets needed was both strong and abiding. In the latter part of the nineteenth century he was a member of the Acclimatisation Society which promoted the establishment of the Brisbane Botanical Gardens and greatly encouraged ventures in agriculture. Working in co-operation with them, James soon showed what could be grown successfully in the North. At Excelsior he grew, not only the plants normally associated with the tropics, but successfully produced crops of peaches (especially the delicious flat Chinese variety), apricots and nectarines, grapes, cherries, English mulberries, quinces and pomegranates.[16]

Tropical products abounded. He had several varieties of mangoes, guavas, mangosteen, lychees, pawpaws, pines, bananas and passionfruit as well as just about every variety of citrus from the giant pomelos to the much tinier limes. He successfully grew both English and sweet potatoes among his vast vegetable patch as well as cocoa, coffee and (black) tea. Dates, coconuts, peanuts and Queensland (Macadamia) nuts flourished as did a variety of spices including both black and white pepper. Sugar cane, which James listed as 'red bamboo', did well as did crops of tobacco, corn and lucerne, rice and the cotton from which the bushes in town had descended. With boundless enterprise he imported and successfully grew Patchouli or Indian Scent bush, from which enchanting perfumes were made. He grew Annotto (or Arnotto) as early as 1881 and processed it to obtain a yellow vegetable dye from the seeds and waxy pulp. This organic dye could be used for colouring fabrics and foodstuff and was also used in lacquers and varnishes. A southern cheese company wrote James a glowing letter of recommendation for the much improved colour of their product after using his vegetable dye. It was also used to enhance the colour of butter.

With tropical fevers unfortunately present in the district, James grew Chinchona from which quinine is produced. Chinchona was a small tree which grew in Peru. A Spanish noblewoman, the Countess of Chinchon[17], contracted a serious fever in Peru and was miraculously cured by a local brew of the chinchona bark. Her recovery was so swift and complete that she willingly gave her name to the healing bark.

The Old Gardens

Across from our house in Furneaux Street was another of my favourite haunts. I didn't know what it had been previously as it had reverted to natural bushland but here and there was evidence of the European touch. Stone borders and circles, a little bridge and even a circular rock arrangement protecting a small spring which exited and flowed under the little bridge. It was all rather enchanting and it wasn't until many years later, when they were restored (without the little spring – the huge melaleucas had drunk it dry), that I found they had been botanical gardens made in honour of Cook's botanist, Sir Joseph Banks. On one of my walks I found a most unusual flower for those times. In the deep shade of the leafy overhang it glowed a striking incandescent red like a ruby. I picked

16 Alan J. Dick *Peninsula Pioneer. James Dick (1849-1916)*Brisbane, 2003.

17 *The Century Dictionary and Encyclopedia* The Century Co., N.Y. 1891

it and took it home to show Mum. She immediately sent me off to the hospital to the doctor's wife, Mrs. Kesteven who quickly looked up her reference books and told me that it was a Billbergia or Bromeliad and had come from Mexico. I was certainly impressed. Mrs. Kesteven had quite a reputation as a garden lover and, taking advantage of her southern connections, used to airfreight trays of the lovely frangipanni flowers that grew at the hospital to a Melbourne florist friend. They were hard to get in those days and in great demand, especially for wedding bouquets.

Local Identity, Miss Eichorn

One day, when there was no riding to look forward to, Dad asked me to take a packet out to Miss Eichorn for him. I had heard about her from the boys. A real weirdo. Lived alone and hated men, except for my father. She was supposed to be a scion of the old German aristocracy and was entitled to put a 'Von' in front of her surname, Caroline Von Eichorn. She had been conducting some business over the family estate in Germany and Dad, as a Justice of the Peace, was helping with the convoluted paperwork. He was intending to take the papers out himself but he had to adjudicate on a court case. I could take his push-bike as Miss Eichorn lived some distance from town on the road past the aerodrome.

Dad gave me detailed instructions on how to get to Miss Eichorn's but I was more than a little bewildered when I pedalled up to the 'X' on the pencilled map Dad drew for me. In the middle of nowhere was a little galvanised hut on low blocks. It was surrounded, not by the usual garden of tropical plants and shrubs, but by piles of galvanised iron and wooden fruit-cases overflowing with bottles and tins. The 'house' seemed to comprise of two rooms – kitchen and bedroom? – and verandah. I couldn't be sure as I only ever got as far as the verandah. I gave Miss Eichorn the packet and as soon as she was assured that I was, truly, my father's daughter, I was treated as an honoured guest. She guided me to a deckchair on the verandah which was decorated, Mad Caroline fashion, with towering piles of newspapers plus the now-expected crates of bottles and tins.

Once I was settled in the deckchair, wedged between two shoulder-high piles of newspapers, Miss Eichorn disappeared into the dark inner room to re-appear with a tray covered with a tatty lace runner, two small fine china cups of strong black coffee and slices of one of the most delicious fruitcakes I had ever tasted. It was her Christmas cake, made from an old family recipe. Once she convinced herself that I wasn't there to find fault and to denigrate her little kingdom, she became quite expansive. The collection of tins and bottles were for 'when they build the factory'. She, too, was an admirer of James Dick and other agricultural pioneers of the area and saw a rosy future for a facility which could add further value to the fruits of the land. Both local fruit and vegetables could be canned and jams, preserves, chutneys and delectable sauces produced for southern and overseas markets. She quite carried me away with her enthusiasm. I thought it all a wonderful idea and was quite sorry to have to leave and ride home.

Dad's court case went off quite well, or so John, one of my friends told me later. It concerned an assault case. The defendant, not known to me, was a patron of the bar at the Middle Pub and quite a peaceful, inoffensive type. For some reason, over the past few weeks, a newcomer had singled him out, ridiculing him and making him the butt of rather tasteless abuse. Finally, the insults got the better of his judgment and he retaliated with a masterly right to the jaw, knocking his tormentor to the floor. Unfortunately, his timing was wrong. The new Policeman had just walked in and the assailant was placed under arrest. John, with a few of his mates who were present at the disturbance, followed up the fun by attending the trial. Both sides of the altercation were aired and my father gave his decision. There was no doubt, he said, that the defendant had been sorely provoked over a lengthy period. However, the same witnesses also stated that he had assaulted his oppressor and my father must find him guilty of the charge. Because of the attenuating circumstances he would fine him the minimum charge – five pounds. At this, John recalled with an appreciative chuckle, the defendant thrust a ten pound note at Dad and said, 'Can I hit him again?' Dad never mentioned the case at home and I didn't get the chance after I'd heard John's story to quiz him. But I thought it not a bad tale.

A – Nursing I'm To Go

Now that we were into the New Year, 1947, Mum was concerned about my future. 'Do you intend to spend the rest of your life riding round with the local yokels?' I should have known better when I made my reply. Among other things, my mother and I didn't share the same sense of humour. On the outer Court House wall was a colourful new poster. I'd helped George put it up. It showed, in the foreground, a noble young woman in white, wearing the proud veil of a nursing sister. Behind it was a schoolgirl, still in uniform, addressing her loving mother. Without a thought of the consequences, I quoted the poster's caption, 'Mother, when I leave school, I want to be a nurse.' 'Good,' Mum immediately replied to my discomfiture, 'I'll get in touch with Matron Keenan straight away.'

One of my aunts had been a nurse and nursing had run in the family. In those days, if a young woman felt that she had to have a paid job, there were only two choices open to her – teaching or nursing, both were considered acceptable professions. Matron Keenan was an old acquaintance of Mum's. She was now matron at the Bundaberg General Hospital, a hospital with the reputation of being one of the State's top training hospitals. In those days, nursing training wasn't a university course. The educational requirement was 'Scholarship (the final year of primary school) standard' and the training was a combination of four year's practical experience with annual exams to check the knowledge gained. I was to begin training at the end of March. With a bit of luck, there was still time for my longed-for visit to Ruth at Butcher's Hill. I think Dad was as taken aback by my 'decision' as I was, but nursing was a highly respected profession, and the knowledge gained would always be of value no matter what life had in store.

I managed to get a letter to Ruth to warn her that I hoped to be out in a fortnight's time with Norman Watkin on his mail run. Dad got me a lift in a truck to Helenvale with another Norman – Norman Palmer. I'd spend the night at Helenvale and leave with Norman Watkin and the mail the following day. Alan suggested that I take Creamy's saddle and bridle 'just in case'and to take my gear, a couple of changes of riding clothes and two dresses, undies, towel and toiletries, in a swag. I followed his advice.

Norman's mother, then Mrs. Watkin but later, Mrs. Leary, put me up for the night at the Lion's Den and got Norman and I away at first light next morning with a tasty breakfast. Norman lent me one of his horses to ride and two horses, packed with mailbags and urgent station supplies and our two swags as top-loads, accompanied us. It was exhilarating riding along through the greener than green countryside though I suspect Norman thought it all rather routine and ordinary. We called at Christensen's at King's Plains with their mail. Norman would pick up any return mail from a 'roadside' drum mailbox the next day. From King's Plains, well-fortified with a meal and hospitality, we crossed first the East and then the West, Normanby Rivers and were at Springvale. We didn't delay there, as at that time only a caretaker was in residence and rode on to Butcher's Hill, arriving before dark.

Butcher's Hill At Last

Our welcome was very warm at our final destination. Ruth, with sister Joyce home on holidays, seemed pleased to see me and introduced me to their mother. She was all that I had imagined and I immediately felt at home. Mrs. Wallace had prepared a delicious meal on the wood stove in the kitchen and while we young ones, joined by Charlie Wallace's righthand man, Jack Doolan, discussed what had been happening both in town and on the station, the older Wallaces retired to the office with the mailbag. Norman had also brought out a smallish parcel of English potatoes and onions for Mrs. Wallace but the Aboriginal 'girl', Nellie, had already taken charge of them and put them in the large store-room that adjoined the dining room. Nellie and her man, Mickey, were eating their meal in their own dining room, the verandah that turned the corner of the kitchen from the shower room, past the laundry bench, to the store-room door. Nellie and Mickey slept in a room at the end of the saddle-shed. There had been roomier quarters along the houseyard fence but since Peter died (and Mrs. Wallace buried him) no one would live there and it had reverted in part to storage space.

Nellie washed up the plates she and Mickey used as well as the pots and pans used for cooking. Joyce, assisted by Jack, attended to our washing-up while we others sat at the table, emptied another pot of black tea and played 'hill-billy' records on the wind-up gramophone. The washer-uppers soon re-joined us and Mr. and Mrs. Wallace returned having gone through their mail. The Boss left us again and went back to the office to write cheques for a couple of accounts. Norman would take them back with him in the morning.

Mrs. Wallace took the kerosene light from the table and we followed her very willingly to the lounge where she entertained us with her talented piano playing. When she and the Boss finally retired closer to town, she gave lots of people much pleasure by playing for the local dances and social events. Norman and Jack left us to have a few 'men's business' words with the Boss, but, as he was a believer in 'early to bed , early to rise', in a short while they joined us again at the piano. It was a wonderful way to end the day and though I was starting to feel rather sleepy, it was a bit sad when Mrs. Wallace closed the lid of the piano and told us it was time we were all in bed.

I slept in a stretcher bed in Ruth's room at the end of the verandah. We were both soon in dreamland but were up to join the rest for an early breakfast in the kitchen. It didn't take Norman long to get his horses ready for the return trip with the mail and two dozen very well-wrapped in large milk tins for his mother. I was pretty sure I'd heard a rooster crow and seen signs of chooks at Helenvale but I guess that, when you run a pub as well as a home, extra eggs are always welcome. The saddle, bridle and saddlecloth Alan lent me were put on 'my' little saddle rack, a smooth tea tree rail jutting out at rightangles from the saddle shed's inner wall. There was a long row of these 'racks' for each rider's saddle, and at the end, for the packsaddles.

We saw Norman off and Ruth made plans for the day. There was no mustering planned. The men were repairing the crush at the yards which had been damaged by a recalcitrant bull. After we'd done a few chores around the house, Mrs. Wallace suggested that the girls take me for a walk down to the Spring. We were accompanied by the Boss's latest idea, two beagle hounds supposed to keep the wallabies from the improved pasture paddocks around the homestead. Butcher's Hill was in a well-watered part of the basaltic country about 80 kilometres in from Cooktown and the homestead was situated between the Spring and the larger Boggy Creek. Visiting Lakeland, as most of Butcher's Hill has now become, I was taken for a drive by daughter Laura to show me a friend's beautiful home built of the local basalt. Near their turn-off was a sign that said, 'Cooktown 85K'. I was amazed. It seemed so much further. A two-day trip then by horse, even when the road opened it still took a full day – at least – to get to town.

On our way down to the Spring, Ruth pointed out a small rise to our left. That was where the unfortunate Peter was buried. The Spring was quite a beauty spot. It was only a small round waterhole from which a narrow streamlet meandered through mossy rocks but it was fed by a perfect little waterfall that cascaded, showily, from well over head-height to the pool at its base. On the bank was a rusted old pump. It was, the girls said, a hydraulic ram. Their great-grandfather, James Earl, who took up Butcher's Hill in the Palmer River goldrush days, had it installed to pump water to supply the old homestead and his extensive garden patch. As well as the mandatory vegetables and fruit trees he grew corn and lucerne for his horses. By some mechanically smart arrangement using an air-chamber and ball-valve, the power of the cascading water was harnessed to lift the captured and piped water well above the height of the crest of the waterfall. It was a very ingenious invention. A lime and a mango tree on the bank were the only survivors of the vegetable patch. The 'new' homestead received its water by windmill and high storage tank from a well beside the house. From it Mrs Wallace, aided by Nellie, watered her flourishing vegetable garden and the ferns and ornamental shrubs that lined the walkway connecting the kitchen/dining room to the main house. In the days of wood stoves, kitchens were often built a little away from the living quarters. Every station had its sweet potato patch (and gangs of marauding bandicoots) and pumpkins were planted every year after the first storms arrived. It was a single planting and the pumpkins were gathered and stored for use throughout the year.

Ruth's Brothers

Ruth and Joyce had two brothers. Hardy, older than Joyce, had served in the Air Force during the war and was now managing a property in the Mt. Garnet area. The younger brother, Billy, in between Joyce and Ruth in age, was on a station further north, Lakefield, which bordered the shores of Princess Charlotte Bay. The Boss owned it , too, in partnership with Bryan Grogan. It was a much bigger area than Butcher's Hill and a lot more isolated but was very good cattle country. Each year, bullocks were brought down by the drovers. Some went on to Mareeba saleyards, others were left at Butcher's Hill to grow out another year and the rest were taken down the track through Daintree to Mossman where the Grogans had butcheries. I was disappointed Billy wasn't home. From the boys in Cooktown I'd heard his praises sung so often. He seemed to hold little short of hero status to all of them. 'Wonderful horseman, first rate cattleman and a top bloke.' I was a little disappointed but there were plenty of things to see and to do.

Ruth was suitably impressed with my leggings but insisted on rubbing them with a rag smeared in melted bullock fat and hanging them in the sun until the grease was absorbed by the dry leather. It worked. They seemed much softer. Mrs. Wallace and Nellie came, at Ruth's request, to have a look at the unusual wrap-arounds. Nellie was quite taken with them and tentatively stroked them with her fingertips. Mrs. Wallace had seen old photos of white Mounted Police officers wearing something very like them with their encircling straps. She was right. Later, looking for photos of Cooktown in the old goldrush period, I found one of a group of mounted Native Police assembled at their Cooktown base. It was the allotment behind the Court House, with the captivating shed and well.

A Ringer's Life

Ruth wore springside leggings, easy to put on and comfortable. Joyce, too. Mrs. Wallace, when she rode out with us, wore the formal top-boots of her show-riding days. No matter what horse she rode, she could always outpace us at a walk. She could get the very best out of her mount at all times. Unfortunately, my leggings didn't have a very long second life. One of the straps, perished no doubt with age, broke. Its tip hung almost to the ground as I was riding Flame, a bright chestnut pony of about fourteens hands in height. Undaunted, I hooked the dangling end 'safely' in the saddle dee on the pommel of my saddle and clean forgot all about it until it was time to dismount. I swung one leg to the ground but the other, hitched to the saddle dee, refused to follow. Flame began to object rather ungraciously. Ruth tried to grab her head but she eluded her. Luckily the frail strap broke and I was able, rather unsteadily, to stand on my two feet. Ruth lent me her discarded 'pull ons' and Nellie, still entranced with the strange-looking leggings, took my discarded ones to 'fix 'im for Mickey'. I don't know if she ever did. Or cared.

One of our first rides, and one where Mrs. Wallace joined us, was to get in some mares to put with the stallion. The station, as was usual practice, bred its own horses. This was done with a strong Thoroughbred bloodline to produce both good stockhorses like the old Australian Waler and for handy gallopers to take to the annual Picnic Races at Laura and Cooktown. Often the best stockhorses doubled as the best racehorses. For the most part of the year, the stallion lived a hermit's life in a small paddock near the stockyards. In the years of Picnic Racing there was very little paperwork required for horses to be eligible to nominate at the meetings. They had to be registered, with their colour, markings (blaze, star, white foot etc) and brands marked on a pictured horse on their certificate together with particulars of age, breeding and their owner's identity. Unlike the more professional guidelines now, foals didn't have to be born as close to August 1st, the horse's official 'birthday', as was possible. It was local practice to wait until good storms fell at the end of the year before paddocking the mares with the stallion. Their personal relationships from then on were left entirely up to them – unless a particularly jealous mare objected to the stallion sharing his affections. With this timing, foals usually didn't appear until about a year later when the storms had again greened the grasslands. Once the mares appeared to be safely in foal, they could be turned back onto their home runs and were not usually mated again until the foal was about a year old and weanable. This left a gap of about two years between matings. Everyone was excited to see the new foals arrive. Colt or filly? What colour?

We alternated our riding horses but, despite the legging episode, Flame was still my favourite. Ruth's was Sunshine, a flashy chestnut with a big, blazed face and four long white stockings. She had a dash of Arab blood and showed it in her lively temperament and broad forehead, huge dark eyes and a head tapering to a nose with flaring nostrils. Joyce's pick was Actress, a dark brown thoroughbred with impeccable manners. I wasn't the only one who nearly came to grief over a bout of vanity. Ruth and Sunshine both loved to show off. At a touch of the reins and a gentle nudge of Ruth's heels, Sunshine would rear straight up, mane and tail flying like the hero's mount in a Western movie. One day, Ruth was to demonstrate how Sunny would rear and place her fore-hoofs on the summit of one of the giant magnetic antbeds common to the area. Sunshine obliged but unfortunately, a couple of heavy storms had softened the usually rock-hard texture of the termite nest and Sunny's front legs almost disappeared into it. Fortunately again, Ruth jumped off, the antbed obligingly crumbled and Sunny was free with nothing hurt save for the antbed and, maybe, Ruth's pride.

As far as Peninsula cattle stations went in the middle of the twentieth century, Butcher's Hill was considered to be 'well improved'. With no road, it was more than just difficult to procure heavy coils of wire for fencing and the far bulkier windmills, storage water-tanks and troughing to equip wells. Around the house and the post and split-rail stockyards (with cattle dip) were small paddocks which made management easier. There was a horse paddock that ran down to Boggy Creek to cater for the horses being worked at the time, the stallion paddock and smaller holding paddocks that could be used for weaners, bulls or any animals that needed to be segregated. The Top Paddock, through which the horse track to Mareeba, as well as the 'road' to Laura, passed, was large enough to be used as a stud paddock where a special bull could run with a select harem to produce a few herd bulls for home use.

Cattle and Cattle Buyers

After the rain, the cattle spread out to take advantage of all the new grass, especially the short, sweet feed that came up in the foothills with the early storms. With the cattle spread out foraging, mustering took considerably longer and, unless, cattle were needed for a special purpose, general mustering was deferred until after the Wet when cattle moved back onto the rivers and water-courses. Bullocks were then mustered and paddocked and the new batch of calves branded. The first week of May usually saw the advent of the cattle buyer from Queerah meatworks in Cairns. Dressed in his stockman's pants, two-pocketed shirt, Akubra hat and boots he looked very much like the general run of ringers though possibly a bit cleaner, better-groomed and with, maybe, the trace of an ironed crease to his sleeves. When a deal was made, a drover would take the cattle, sometimes combined with other neighbouring 'fats', to the railhead at Mareeba. Mareeba had both saleyards and the Bacon Factory which also slaughtered cattle. Cattle destined for the larger meatworks in Cairns were trucked down by rail.

It was too early in the year to muster bullocks but, having killed before Christmas, Mrs. Wallace was suggesting with feeling that it was time to 'get a killer in'. The Boss, assisted by Jack, Ruth and me set off to find a suitable 'killer'. Speyed (de-sexed) cows were popular. They were usually old breeder cows speyed because of age. Once denied the doubtful joys of reproduction and the rearing of calves , they responded by rapidly putting on weight. This 'new' meat was tender but it also had the advantage of the increased flavour of 'aged' meat. A suitable killer was found, brought in with a few mates for 'coachers' so that she wouldn't 'stir up'. One shot from the Boss's faithful .22 was enough. While the men set about skinning her and cutting the carcase into more manageable quarters, Ruth and I turned the others back onto their run. With not even a kerosene fridge at that time, very little fresh meat could be kept. Even with the greatest care taken, meat in the Coolgardie safes kept cool by a drip system, had to be consumed within two or three days. During that time we feasted on steak, liver, brains, sweet-bread and fresh roasts. The rest of the meat was dry-salted. Cut into manageable pieces it was scored with a few knife cuts and rubbed carefully with the dry, coarse salt. As each piece was salted it was stacked on the bench in the fly-gauzed meat-house or butcher shop, and 'turned' changing the top layer to the bottom each morning and evening for several days when the beef showed signs of drying-out.

It was then hung on fencing-wire hooks from a rail in the butcher shop and left there until daily inspection proved it to be 'cured'. It was then bagged or boxed ready for use. If the weather was overly wet and humid, prolonging the salt-preservation, the salted pieces could be finished off by smoking in the little galvanised iron smoke-house behind the butcher shop. Smoking gave it quite an agreeable smoky flavour. Very, very little of the beast was wasted. The dogs relished the bones, as did the chooks. The guts and non-usable offal made good pig food and even the manure –contents of the rumen and stomach –were made welcome by Mickey who carted it off to the vegetable garden. Often, the gut was cured, too, as tripe. All fat was rendered down in a boiler on the kitchen stove. The best was kept for dripping for use in the house for cooking. Butter was often too precious to be used in any but the most special cakes and fat, with a squeeze of lemon juice, was the usual 'shortening' in recipes. With the addition of caustic lye, fat was also the main ingredient for huge rectangles of soap cut into bars for laundry purposes

The hide was kept, usually as greenhide which had many uses. It made hobble-straps, plaited or twisted ropes and could even make a passable mattress base for bush timber stretcher beds. At times, the hide was tanned to provide leather for saddle repairs. The local ironwood bark was used as a tanning agent. Possibly, after seeing the state of my ill-fated leggings, Jack had a bright idea to get neat's foot oil. I don't know how successful he was, but he appropriated the long leg bones, hoofs and joints for his purpose. There was also talk of 'bone marrow'.

It seemed to be no time at all from when he'd brought me out, that Norman arrived again with the mail. There was a letter for me, too. From Dad. My holidays were to come to an end. Alan would be out in a week's time to escort me back to town. Joyce assured me I'd enjoy nursing. Mrs. Wallace backed that up and told how her sister, Mona, had acted as hospital matron for years and regretted having to leave, as was the rule, when she married. Ruth was a bit wary about all this nursing talk. Nursing was something she was threatened with if stories came back of her exploits in town. Her father said they'd have to send her a lot further away than the Mareeba Hospital to train. She'd be back with the first returning drover's plant.

The Ride Back to Cooktown

Mrs. Wallace, Joyce and Ruth were determined that my last days with them would be most enjoyable. We went for a few short rides to see the Cooktown orchids in bloom in the 'scrub' and to visit a couple of pretty little waterfalls further away from the house. On one occasion, Joyce, Ruth and I had taken the horses down to a favourite swimming hole in Boggy Creek and were having fun in its cool, clear water when a horseman rode up. It was Alan. Creamy was waiting in the Nighthorse Paddock at the homestead. We'd get a daylight start the next day.

Nellie had lit the stove and Mrs. Wallace prepared breakfast as Alan caught the horses and saddled them ready to leave. The sun was just rising above the horizon. It was hard to say goodbye to the family as they lined up to wave and to see us off. I wished Dad and Gran could have shared my holiday with me. They'd have loved it. Dad knew Ruth's mother and had a high opinion of her multi-faceted ability. She was the one who attended to the station's paperwork and dealt with officials as well as carrying out her station duties.

It was good to mate up again with Creamy and the horses, homeward bound, made short work of the road to Springvale. We didn't call in but saw someone who waved to us from the little spring on the right hand side of the road. Alan knew who it was, an old prospector, and said he had washed a bit of fine gold from the spring, enough to half-fill an old-time glass junket-tablet tube , a favourite gold-dust receptacle. We pulled up to boil our quartpots and eat Mrs. Wallace's sandwiches on the shady bank of the West Normanby River, a pleasant spot but we couldn't linger. The East Normanby was crossed at Hahl's Crossing. In the goldrush days, Ted Hahl had a raftlike contraption there on which he used to ferry travellers and their gear- even buggies - over the river. A couple of old mango trees on the east bank marked the site of his hut and some tobacco plants, a relic of the Chinese gardeners, grew wild further along the bank. During the tobacco shortage in the war years the long ride out from Cooktown to pick the leaf was considered very worth the while. Adjoining Ted's place, upstream a little, were a few ancient posts, all that remained of the Police Paddock where the old-time Mounted Police held their horses while on patrol. We rode past what remained of Harvest Home and its sad graves on our left and, to our right, a lovely little lagoon covered in lilac waterlilies and foraging waterbirds. Our night camp, King's Plains, was near at hand. We crossed a tiny wooden bridge and turned off the track that we were following to go in to King's Plains.

Glady and Jock knew we were coming. Alan had called in on his way to pick me up. Jock left with Alan to attend to the horses and I went with my hostess to take a bath (using a bedroom jug and basin set) before we sat down to tea. The King's Plains house then was the one the Gibsons had built in the early days. It was of pit-sawn boards, secured by the 'drop-slab'method in deep grooves cut into the uprights. Pit-sawing produced very useful timber but being the man on the end of the saw at the bottom of the pit over which the log to be cut was placed couldn't have been very enjoyable. The bedroom floors were of Leichhardt, a big, shady tree that grew along the watercourses. Its timber, especially when scrubbed with home-made caustic soap, was almost white. Glady showed me to the bed with its cast-iron scrolled head and foot in the spare bedroom while Alan unrolled his swag on the kitchen verandah.

King's Plains, the Christensens and Christy Palmerston

The kitchen was a separate building connected by a 'covered way' to the main house. It had an enormous double-oven range that must have taken up a lot of space on the wagon that brought it out from the wharf at Cooktown. One oven was for cooking, the other was a warming oven. There was an antbed floor in the kitchen, less likely to ignite should a stray coal fall. It was so well swept and watered that it looked more like smooth cement. We sat around the long bush-made table, Jock on a chair at the head and the three of us ranged either side on long forms that ran the length of the table. The tea-pot was kept full and we talked and listened well past the normal time to turn-in. Glady and Jock told us the story of King's Plains connection with a colourful goldrush figure, Christy Palmerston. Christy had found himself in trouble with the Geraldton (now Innisfail) Mining Warden over claims and counterclaims of assault and robbery on the Russell River field, between the present Innisfail and Gordonvale. The ratio of Chinese to European was high in the Asians favour and caused no little resentment by miners alleging that the Warden favoured the Chinese over the Europeans. Palmerston, after being summoned peremptorily to the Warden's office on charges of assault on several Chinese miners, was ordered to be 'bound over to keep the peace'.[18]Christy thought that the easiest way to do that was to leave the turbulent goldfield and to make himself scarce. He hid out on Mt. Byerley, a mountain between King's Plains and Harvest Home. While living in seclusion there, Mrs. Henderson of Mareeba, then the young daughter of Hugh Sampson Douglas of Harvest Home, would take him food prepared by her mother. According to the Christensens, Palmerston's outlawry ended when a meeting was arranged by the King's Plains Gibsons between the fugitive and

18 Warden's report, Geraldton. December 1887

the Mining Warden from Cooktown. They met at the very table around which we were sitting. The result was that Christy Palmerston felt free to return to his mining and path-finding occupations. As far as I have been able to find out, this is only a local story but the Christensens for whom Palmerston held hero status, were sure it did happen. When they built a new home closer to the lagoon, they pulled down the white-ant eaten old building but left the kitchen standing as a memorial to a man not unduly known as the 'Prince of Pathfinders'.

Today, the road turns south from the old turn-off and heads past what used to be the Plain, a great expanse of open grassland through which the silvery water of the Lakes were easily visible, and on to Helenvale. The Plain has now been covered in re-growth and you can no longer see the Lakes. That road was longer than the old wagon road to Cooktown by way of the Oakey. Early next morning we took the Oakey route, the old Douglas Track from The Palmer to Cooktown. Not long after leaving King's Plains we rode past the barely visible remains of what Alan said was the old hotel at Deep Creek before coming to the first of the Oakey Creek crossings. The Oakeys all run into the Annan River and there are several crossings of the branches. At Middle Oakey were more derelict posts and a few sheets of tangled iron, relics of yet another hotel and Hamilton, a goldrush township.

Once past the Oakeys we didn't have far to ride to get to the more visible road from the northern farmlands to Cooktown. We arrived home in good time. Alan retrieved my swag and left the horses to recover from their exertions in the back yard while he had tea with us. It was fun being able to recount the highlights of our ride and my wonderful stay with the Wallaces, but, for some reason, I felt terribly tired and wasn't all that sorry when Alan said his goodnights and we retired to our beds.

A-Nursing I Shall Go

Dad arranged for my boat ticket and booked a sleeper on the train to Bundaberg. When the time all too quickly came, he took me down to catch the launch and, in parting. gave me a goodbye hug and kiss, told me to 'Be good', predicted that I'd like my new life once I settled in and pressed a small parcel into my hand just as we had to part. I confess it was with teary eyes that I opened it after I'd waved goodbye to Dad's disappearing figure on the little wharf. The brown paper covering revealed a watch with a second hand, so necessary for nurses taking pulse and respiration counts, and a precious five pound note ($10). A friend of my parents picked me up from the launch in Cairns , put up with me for the night and cordially escorted me to the train the next day. All the while they assured me that I'd really like nursing, make a lot of friends and gain knowledge that would be an advantage even if I didn't make nursing a life-long career.

An Introduction to Nursing

Despite a sneaky feeling of adventure, it was sad to be leaving the North. A woman with a small child joined me south of Cairns. She was going to Townsville so I had congenial company to take my mind off my sorrows. I was getting to be quite an expert on the railway and recognised the towns and the approaches to them as we chugged along the route, sharing my knowledge, whether they liked it or not, with my fellow travellers. With some trepidation I left the train at Bundaberg knowing that there was no one there to meet me. Luckily, the taxi driver who took me to the hospital was most helpful. He pointed out the main reception desk, carried my bag in for me and informed the woman there that I was the new nurse from Cooktown. I was taken to Matron Keenan's office where she arranged for a senior nurse to take me to the nurses' quarters and to show me the ropes. I had a day off to collect my uniforms and get what I needed and report for duty at a quarter to six the following morning in Ward IV, the Male Ward.

It was all a bit too much to take in but, after introducing me to some of the other girls – there were close to twenty in my 'year' – I found that my nurse escort came from Monto. One of my mates at Girls Grammar was a Monto girl. My guide knew Gwen. She was her sister. Being about two years older than us, she had only a little over twelve months of her training to go. The senior theatre nurse also had a sister who was at Grammar during my time there. I was beginning to feel more at home. Some girls were locals but the majority were bush-bred girls from a wide area of the State, from cattle and sheep stations, dairies and farms. One of the first priorities was to get my uniforms. Matron had alerted that department so it was just a matter of selecting one of the willing guides to show me where to go. In no time, I'd tried on the white, button-through uniform with its short sleeves, Peter Pan collar and top pocket. 'Keep it on,' my friend and the kindly staff advised me and adjusted the starched nurse's cap on my hair (short, 'above collar' length and 'confined'. No stray strands falling seductively over the face.) It was secured with a couple of strong, strategically placed, bobby pins and I was given a glimpse of Nurse Waddell in the full-length mirror. A small vertical strip of royal blue on the turn-back of the cap indicated that I was 'first' year. Luckily, Mum had known about the required footwear and bought the 'sensible' laced tan shoes and some lisle stockings. I was already wearing the former to 'break them in' and the latter were safe in my suitcase. The women handed me two more uniforms, all marked with my name and we were free to go back to the quarters.

First year nurse's pay wasn't all that generous, one pound sixteen shillings and six pence a fortnight or less than $2 a week, but Mum had already told me how, as she was growing up and nursing was considered as a possible career, her father had to pay the hospitals to train her two older sisters. Our uniforms, their laundering and repair were the hospital's responsibility and we had full board and lodging provided. In colder weather we wore either the traditional short, red cape or a red cardigan over our uniforms. The cleaning of these, as was that of our undies and 'civvy' clothes, our responsibility.

Once back in my little cubicle-like room, a door opening from the internal corridor, another onto the long verandah that skirted the quarters, on my new friends' advice, I kept my uniform on, added the flesh-coloured stockings and hung my spare uniforms in the small combined wardrobe/dressing table. My bed and a small wooden chair completed the furniture. My fellow-nurses helped me unpack and the animated conversation came to a sudden stop at the sound of a bell. Dinner!There was a rush for the large dining room, situated in the very centre of the hospital complex on the top floor. On the far side of the dining room was the Lady Chelmsford, the separate maternity hospital. We shared the dining room, but not the individual tables. The obstetric nurses sat on their side, we on ours.

I had a few trepidations about starting off in the Male Ward. With no brothers and with my horsey mates being extremely decorous – they wouldn't dream of taking a shirt off in my presence even on the hottest and most humid of tropical days – I was having second thoughts about my ability to give a male an all-over wash, even if he were bedridden. I needn't have worried and, under the expert tutelage of my fellow nurses I could soon make beds with creaseless draw-sheets and precise mitred corners and the bed-baths and the back-rubs were a breeze.

Memorable Patients

Hospital stays in those days were longer but we had quite a turn-over of patients in the wards. It was the days of Queensland's rightly famous 'free hospitals'. On the verandahs were the more permanent cases, men who would now be residents in aged care homes. They were old hands at the hospital game and were well aware of the advent of a raw, new trainee. One old fellow I found a particular trial. He seemed to wait until I was on duty to play up. Taking the tea-trolley around one afternoon, his bed was empty. 'Go and find him,' was Sister's immediate, icy order. Two of us quickly scouted the wards and bathrooms without sighting him. Even a look under the low-stumped floor, refuge on some nights for wild pigs being hunted on the banks of the adjacent Burnett River, revealed nothing. Then I noticed a movement in the front garden, in the rose bed. There he was, in a striped pyjama top, no pants, serenely picking a bunch of roses. We quickly got him back inside and into his cast-off trousers but getting him into bed wasn't as simple. The roses were for Sister. He wanted to present them to her. Sister's previous desire to have him transferred to a home had a temporary set-back as she thanked him delightedly for the beautiful flowers and the kind thought.

We, on the other hand, were extremely negligent. He should have been better supervised. We would be held responsible if something like that happened again. She did, however, agree to equip his bed with safety rails, two long sets which were anchored to both sides of the bed to prevent patients from inadvertently rolling over and onto the floor. Only a few evenings later when I was working a late shift until 9.30, it started again. I felt that he knew I was inexperienced and hence, vulnerable. We'd just settled everyone in for the night, lights were dimmed, silence prevailed and, in Sister's office, the night staff were reading the report ready to take over. Suddenly, there was a commotion, much metal-rattling and shouting. Sitting up in bed, he passionately attacked the bed-rails, yelling, 'Mary, where's the bloody gate?' Luckily it was time for the night staff to take over and I think the two whispering Sisters decided that a mild sedative was in order. We day-staffers made ourselves scarce.

He was supposed to drink 'copious' fluids for his condition but this didn't suit our favourite patient. Any tea or cocoa I brought him was undrinkable. The same went for the water in his water jug when I tried to persuade him to try a draught of that. The Deputy Matron, an ex-Army Sister, had an idea. Mandarins were ripe in everybody's back yard. Matron arranged for one of his occasional visitors to bring in a dozen. They were huge, loose-skinned golden beauties. Matron came to do her rounds. As Junior Nurse, I was to accompany her and Sister as general dogsbody. When we reached my favourite patient, my heart stood still. On his bed table was a dish, full to overflowing with mandarin skins and pips. They should've been removed before Matron's rounds! Matron, however, seemed delighted. Her solution looked like it might be working.

'Oh, Mr. T,' she gushed admiringly. 'Did you eat all those?'

Mr. T. hadn't had a literary background for nothing. Disregarding me for once, he fixed poor Matron with a disapproving scowl and said in his very best clipped-tone voice, 'No, Matron. I *left* all those.'

We spent eight weeks in each ward before moving on to the next. I think I went to the kids' ward, in any case I was no longer in Men's. A phone call one night alerted the same poor Sister who was still in Ward IV. She immediately dispatched two nurses to find Mr. T. His bed was empty. A second phone call was made, from Sister to the Fire Brigade with an admonition to 'bring your longest ladder'. Mr. T. had gone walkabout to the little triangular park and garden at a road intersection just in front of his ward. In the triangle was a very tall, elevated water tank, part of the town supply. He'd taken up the challenge, climbed the precarious ladder snaking up the tank's side and was calling out raucously to passing cars. The Fire Brigade managed to get the uncooperative adventurer down safely. Matron was not amused. This time, Sister was told to be more vigilant but Mr. T., to everyone's relief, his long-suffering relatives included, was immediately found a place in a very reputable Nursing Home in Brisbane.

Those who predicted I'd get to enjoy nursing were, for the most part, right. The nurses and other staff were great to work with. Our 'year' (first) was a bit unusual. We had two ex-Army nurses, Teddy and Audrey, who needed experience nursing women, children and the elderly, to round off their nursing training and to qualify them for a General Nursing registration. A couple of years ahead of us were two English nurses, cousins, whose families had migrated to Australia in the post-war rush. They had both completed three years training and exams in the U.K. but had another year to go to meet Queensland's registration requirements. They were so pleased when they completed the extra time and were given their sister's veils, in recognition of their higher status. In the transfer of their U.K. training they had only lost the six weeks 'probation' at the start of their in-hospital tuition.

Although nurses worked strange hours including a two-month stretch of night duty, Bundaberg's social life was very much alive and well. A small minus was the position of the morgue beside the outside gate to the nurses' quarters. I'd been repeatedly told how off-putting it was to be bidding a fond farewell to the boyfriend when the morgue light would flash on and a draped trolley arrive. The gentlemen usually tore themselves from even the most passionate embrace and promptly left. Fortunately, I never found myself in that predicament. While in Men's Ward I'd helped nurse Vince who was recovering from an operation and, better still, through him, his wife Molly. Molly was another horse-crank. Show horses, hacks, were her forte. Within a few brief meetings at Vince's bedside, I felt as if I'd known her all my life. When she came to take Vince home, she reminded me of her invitation to visit them and hoped that I wouldn't leave it too long.

Back to the Horses

This was easy. Bundy has been called the Bicycle City, though neighbouring Maryborough was also a serious contender for the same title. I think almost every nurse owned a bicycle. I'd bought a second-hand one as soon as I could though it'd cost just over a fortnight's wages. Our bikes gave us wonderful mobility. Molly and Vince lived on a small acreage just on the edge of town on the way to Bargara's beaches. Vince used to break-in amd educate horses and also do farriery work. All this in his 'spare time' for he had a real job at the sugar mill. Molly's horses had a convenient grassy paddock to play in, an exercise yard adjoining the round-yard Vince used for breaking-in, for their education and several comfortable stables to rest in. There was a horse I could ride and, hopefully, not ruin. My move from my Cooktown mates suddenly became less hard to endure. Of course, I had to mention Bessie and her beautiful show horses and, to top it all, not only was Molly also an ardent admirer but she'd also met Bessie while visiting friends at the Toowoomba show. Molly and Vince's place soon became my home for all my off-duty hours. They helped me buy a saddle from a local saddle-maker. A Cox poley, made to measure and light enough for a show saddle, yet with a narrow waist and high-set knee-pads that gave the rider that comforting 'no horse can throw me' feeling. Vin also cut me out a bridle and with Molly's help I was able to sew it together to make a bridle that didn't disgrace my lovely saddle.

Vin was breaking in a young thoroughbred colt for a friend. He was destined for the race track but was, although still a young stallion, endowed with a very loving and lovable nature. Vin let me ride him and I was hooked. He was a tall, chestnut horse, something of the same rich colour as Ruth's Sunshine, with a blaze face and white socks, not as showy as Sunny's long stockings, but none the less eye-catching. Through Molly's fellowship I soon gained entry to the show horse fraternity and with Mort's backing –he owned Ty, the would-be race horse – I was given access to the racing crowd too. This eventually mushroomed into 'riding work', mostly taking Ty with another horse companion for road work, long rides at lower paces, but also included some track work. My weight was by no means jockey-like but I guess willing hands were never rejected.

At the hospital, 'rounds' were done every night at 10p.m. to ensure all trainees were safely home, unless they had a 'late pass' which gave free rein until midnight. Luckily, no check was kept in the early morning hours so important in a racehorse's life. If I took off in my riding gear while it was still dark, I could get some track-riding in before turning up, completely transformed in my nurse's uniform, to read the report at 5.45 a.m. prior to going on duty in the ward.

The Joys of Night Duty

In due course, I had to do my stint of night duty, 9.30 p.m. to 6 a.m.. This interfered with the track-work but gave me plenty of time for afternoon roadwork and trying to learn to educate young horses in the exercise yard with Molly. On my first night duty, Teddy and I were the lowly 'spares', junior nurses required to go wherever they were needed in the wards. We were also responsible for the night staff's meals and the washing-up. This could be difficult, especially if a call came from the ward when our meal was at a strategic point of preparation. It was the custom of night duty spares to leave a note for their successors to pass on any helpful hints. One especially appreciated that winter concerned ham bones in the huge, wall-size refrigerator. Not that the nurses' dining room ever saw ham, except for a little at Christmas. We were given access to a high, top compartment of the fridge. The rest of the refrigerator was locked. By standing on a chair you could fairly easily reach the few pieces of meat, the eggs, milk, butter etc left out for the preparation of our midnight supper. By reaching further in, leaning over the top shelf, it was possible using a long cooking fork to spear any ham bone or other tempting item stashed on the shelf below. The top shelf could be pulled out to make a gap at the back for the midnight robbery. The ham bone made very welcome soup on the colder nights and the pot could safely remain on the range to simmer should we be called to the wards. Potatoes and onions, being everyday staples, weren't kept under lock and key and were available on open racks in the kitchen. We became quite famous for our ham and potato soup. The bone was carefully replaced and we could get up to three chances to use it before it lost its flavour completely.

Teddy was very adept at finding things on the forbidden shelves but one night she found herself faced with the prospect of spending a rather long and nasty night, stuck half in and half out of the fridge. It was her practice to remove her uniform before climbing the chair to perpetrate her cat-burglary. This night she was wearing her night duty special, a rather violently royal blue satin petticoat. As she tried to wiggle a little further into the fridge to investigate the lower shelf, the treacherous chair fell to the floor leaving her dangling half in, half out of the compartment. Teddy retained a rather colourful vocabulary from her Army days and began to use it, at the top of her voice, to summon me, her junior. Unfortunately, I'd been called to one of the wards. I'd gone to the store-room to tell Teddy but she must've been too intent on her search to hear me. As she heard footsteps approaching her voice and vocab increased in intensity until she was firmly grasped about the waist and swung to the floor. Her rescuer, nearly splitting his sides with laughter, was one of the young doctors, returning from a late call to a delivery at the Chelmsford. Fortunately it was our favourite, Humph. I arrived soon after the rescue was effected. Teddy was in her uniform and making coffee – perfectly legitimate, we were left enough for a cup each. – for herself and her Sir Galahad. Humph was a fairly regular visitor to the night kitchen. He seemed to be summoned to late night deliveries much more often than the other junior R.M.Os (Resident Medical Officers) We all liked him and willingly gave him the coffee which he indisputably appreciated. We both knew that our secret pilfering and the news of Teddy's misadventure would be safe with him. It wouldn't stop him laughing about it but he wouldn't report us. He thought the ham bone extrication and our manner of pinching bananas from a hanging bunch through the iron window bars of another locked store room, showed initiative. Of course, he enjoyed the odd banana fritter with his coffee as much as we did.

Humph was our instructor for anatomy and in that capacity marked our completed test papers which were then handed on to Deputy Matron to be passed back to us. At times, his quirky sense of humour got the better of his discretion and he red-pencilled comments in the margin. One I recall was when a nurse confused the Eustachian tube which connects nasal and oral passages with the Fallopian tube that connects ovary and uterus. 'That would, indeed, be an ectopic pregnancy', he commented in red. Unfortunately, Matron noticed it too and forbade him to make any more comments. We missed them, but everyone in our year passed Humph's final exam. We all had our eyes on our favourite R.M.O. but he later married one of the sisters from the Lady Chelmsford and, after some time, moved to a hospital on the Darling Downs.

Teddy's misfortunes for the night didn't end with the ham bone affair. The meal over, I collected the trays from the wards and washed up. Teddy's job was to dry the crockery and cutlery, put them in an antiquated lift arrangement and by pulling the right ropes, deliver them to the staff dining room ready for use at breakfast. It was a hectic night and we were both scurrying from place to place. Coming back from one trip, Teddy hurriedly stacked the washed and dried items in the lift and pulled the ropes. They reached the second floor safely but, before

Teddy could do anything to try to arrest the catastrophe, the whole lot, lift and all, came hurtling down. Smashed china everywhere. 'After I'd washed the b*** things up!' Teddy growled with pent-up fury. She got off lighter than the hapless boilerman's cat. It was a general favourite of both kitchen and night staff. Summer nights were spent hunting mice but in winter he preferred to curl up in one of the warming ovens of the big kitchen ranges. We were all aware of Ginger Tom's habits but one night, a stand-in Night Sister, looking for one of the spares, noticed the open door. Her tidy nature offended, she shut it. Next morning the boilerman was heartbroken. His cat wasn't there to greet him. By the time Tom was found it was too late.

Smallpox Scare

Humph also came in for his share of bad luck. Chickenpox had broken out. Isolation was filled with spotty children and the powers-that-were, fearing a smallpox outbreak, because there was one raging in India, decided we'd all be vaccinated against it. It was to be 'voluntary' as there could be debilitating side effects that included a form of blindness. Despite that, we were all vaccinated, like it or not. The skin of the upper left arm was broken and the vaccine applied. In no time at all, despite the covering dressing, the left arms of 90% of the nursing staff swelled enormously. Half of us found it difficult even to lift our left arms. Work in the wards turned out, perhaps a little less than torture, but definitely with a 'hard labour'effect. Teddy's mate, Audrey, ended up in a darkened cubicle in sickbay for several days until she regained her sight to everyone's thankful relief. Meanwhile, for the doctors, the choice for vaccination was theirs alone. Humph opted not to receive vaccination. It was our turn to laugh when we heard about his predicament. While he was applying the volatile vaccine to the unfortunate nurses' arms, he forgot about a small cut he had near the nail of his right index finger. Unaware of this entry site, he vaccinated himself in the finger which immediately trebled in size and later painfully shed its fingernail before subsiding. At least he was then, like us, vaccinated and smallpox-proof.

The young Resident Medical Officers were discouraged, if not actually banned, from riding motorbikes and even from playing football. Too many unnecessary accidents. I'm sure riding track-work would have come into the same category too, had Matron even suspected it. We all too often saw the carnage caused by motorbikes. Two young men were brought in, both in a critical condition from a motorcycle smash and both of them still under twenty-one. Some of the nurses knew them which made their suffering all the more tragic. One had head injuries. His face was barely recognisable as human and his body was covered in gaping gashes that looked as if they were made by a crazed sabre-wielding assassin. The other patient was much less perturbing to see. He was badly bruised but had none of the horrifying wounds suffered by his mate. Internal injuries.

'Good,' we all thought confident that time and dedicated nursing would soon have him well. The first patient was 'specialled' day and night for several days. It was a labour of love for us all. Every sign of improvement was greeted with both joy and disbelief. We couldn't really believe anyone could survive with such appalling injuries. After weeks of intensive nursing, he did, walked out of the hospital unaided and married a nurse, not one of us who nursed him, but one who met him later at a dance. His friend remained unconscious for days with barely a movement even of his chest to show he still lived. One night, just as the shifts were being changed, the senior nurse monitoring him checked his heart, respiration and listened to his abdomen for signs that the muscular movement of his alimentary canal, peristalsis, was restored. In her excitement at her findings she almost ran into the sisters' office. Incredibly, all readings were very closely back to normal. Mystifyingly, the sisters exchanged sad glances and shook their heads. She was very taken aback by their negative reaction to her good news but, after a brief pause, they returned with her to his bedside. He was completely inert, inanimate, no pulse, no respiration. He had died. The nurse was overcome and the sisters tried to comfort her. They'd seen it all before, a hopeless case suddenly appearing to be restored to normal. It strengthened her belief in the Resurrection, one sister said. We were always overjoyed when our patients recovered but there was also the odd heartbreak when we worried if maybe there could have been something else we could have done.

On The Catwalk

Some light relief came with a fund-raising event. A five star mannequin parade was planned. The shops and more exclusive boutiques were enthusiastic in their support and promotion but they needed more models. Matron agreed that the nursing staff could help and mine was one of the names put forward. I certainly wasn't at all prepared for being one of the two chosen to display the bridal attire. Teddy couldn't believe it either and we finally agreed it must've been my height. The other girl was also taller than average, ideal for long skirts and trailing trains. I had another few moments of glory modeling a New Look 'after five' dress with a captivating mid-calf, swirling silvery grey skirt and a more ordinary, rather modest, sunfrock but I came down to earth quickly on my final appearance on the cat-walk. I was modeling another innovation, pedal-pushers, shorts with much longer, well below the knee, trouser legs. Ideal for bike riding. I wondered how I could get to buy a pair. Thinking lovely thoughts and imagining myself in my very own pedal-pushers, I reached the end of the cat-walk. Directly below me were the Medical Super and his wife. Dr. Scott had, even in normal times, a rather loud voice. On this occasion, the effect was shattering. 'Haw! Haw! Haw!' he guffawed. 'We had an old Chinee gardener wore those pants!'. My desire to own a pair of pedal-pushers immediately evaporated.

Money was always a problem for us nurses. Teddy, being older, ex-Army and much, much wiser, taught us all. After visiting hours we were quick to beat the domestic staff in collecting any empty softdrink bottles left behind. Taken to the corner shop we amassed a penny halfpenny (1.5c) for each bottle. But things were all cheaper in those days.

Polocrosse

Polocrosse was starting to gain favour and Bundaberg established one of the first clubs. Molly and I went to watch and soon became ardent fans. Vin had a chestnut galloway (a big pony or a little horse), Ginger Meggs, that he thought would make a good polocrosse pony. He lent her to me and he was right. She was like a good stockhorse but, instead of 'following a beast' in best stockhorse tradition, she followed the ball. Meggsie seemed to have learnt the rules well before I could absorb them all. She followed that little ball, never taking her eyes off it, slowing almost imperceptively as she came alongside to give me a chance to scoop it up. Once she felt the weight of the ball in the long-handled racquet, she'd flatten her ears back and head at top pace direct for the goal.I decided, against Molly and Vin's remonstration, that I should contribute to Meggsie's feed. She ran in the paddock but had a small feed night and morning to keep her in top condition. Bran was eight shillings (80c) and lucerne chaff, another staple, twelve shillings and sixpence ($1.25) a bag. To finance this habit, I consulted my horse-trainer mates, both Toms. Tom Bavister was an old Cooktownite and knew Dad when he was first there as Warden's Clerk. His brother had one of the first taxis in the town, Dad told me. He nearly came to grief when he drove down along the wharf to meet the just-berthed steamship that plied the coast to Thursday Island each month. Unfortunately, the brakes failed and he and the taxi kept going, to everyone's consternation, over the edge of the pier. Tom agreed with a chuckle that the story was true but added that they 'fished it out' and got it going again.

The Racing Fraternity

Tom wasn't a machinery man. An old bachelor, horses were his love and his life. He had a jockey who used to ride work for him but he kindly let me ride one of his charges (in a real jockey pad) around the stable yard at times and allowed me to help by 'mucking-out' the horses' stalls. If Tom had a certainty, he'd tell me to put five bob (50c) on it. 'Can't be beat.' Usually, every punter agreed with him and 'even money' was generous odds, but it helped pay for Meggsie's feed. Tom had another practice about which I was more than a little uneasy. When he mixed up the evening feed for his top horse, he added a pinch of arsenic. 'As much as will fit on the flat side of a horseshoe nail', Tom demonstrated. He then took a pinch of the powder for himself. With a 'what's good for horse is good for man'. He went on to explain that Cleopatra took arsenic to maintain her ravishing complexion and it didn't kill her. I wasn't that keen on a ravishing complexion and resisted his generous offer.

His horse won the big race Tom was preparing him for – and dropped dead just after passing the winning post. Bundy raced fortnightly in those days but I was unable to go to every meeting. I missed the next one but, in a way, was relieved when I heard the unhappy news. Tom collapsed and died at the rails while watching his other horse come third in its event. The dose must've been pretty much the same for man and horse.

The other Tom was from Gympie and a cousin of my cousins there. We got on well from the start though Teddy disapproved and warned me to take care. He had 'shifty eyes'. Tom said it was a 'cunning look' and necessary when dealing with bookies. All horse-trainers had to have them.

My time was kept over-full with things to do. If I weren't on duty, I'd be on my bike heading out to the horses or else riding. A nursing friend was expecting her brother, coming to Bundaberg for a holiday. He was head stockman on one of the biggest cattle stations in the Gulf. I was impressed. When I actually met him, I was even more so. My friend Pat suggested that I go out with him. He was an ideal companion and tall, dark and handsome as well. We spent any free time that I could scrounge riding or going out to farms for Jack to ride fractious horses. Vin lined these outlaws up for us and sometimes came out, too, to watch and to generally give a hand. Once the horses found out that they couldn't get away with bad behaviour they settled down and minded their manners. The horse-owners were grateful and plied us with cups of tea and farewell gifts of produce. I was so sorry when Jack's holiday was over and I couldn't understand why Pat didn't seem as friendly as usual towards me. Trust Teddy to provide the answer. Pat expected me to act like a well-brought-up young lady and take Jack to the dance hall and the movies. Anything but riding more buckjumpers.

My holidays came around and I went back to Cooktown but it was too wet to organise a trip out to see Ruth. Another exam was ticked off the list and I took my cap to the sewing room to have a second blue stripe added. When possible I rode one of Tom's horses. By this time the gate-keepers at the race-course knew me and with a nod to each other and a muttered 'the nurse', would let me in to the races for nothing. Tom had a new horse he was rather reticent about but at this meeting, a special annual one, he told me to put five bob (50c) on it, straight out for a win. I didn't have Old Tom to consult and was apprehensive as the horse had no performance to recommend it. 'Go on', Tom urged and I reluctantly went up to my usual bookie. The horse was six to one. I didn't back it but went back to Tom to query the price. Those shifty eyes? Was the horse 'in the bag'? A non-trier? 'Put your money on,' said Tom. My betting was still a little in credit so I invested the five shillings. The horse won easily. Tom was congratulated on all sides and I collected my winnings. At six to one, I'd increased five shillings to thirty-five in a matter of minutes. My bike was outfitted with brand new tyres and tubes and I still had some money left over.

Mort decided it was time to put Ty in regular training and Tom was going to take him. Tom came out to Molly and Vin's after smoko. Vin suggested I take Ty and Tom another of the thoroughbreds in Vin's stable and go for a ride. Do a bit of road work down the Bargara road. It sounded great and everything was going fine until, just as we turned to come back, a thunder storm appeared from nowhere and made its presence felt with pelting rain. Beside the road was a farm shed. We decided to shelter there but, just as Tom dismounted to undo the cocky's gate, there was a horrendous flash of lightning and simultaneous loud crack of thunder. Ty reared, almost over backwards and suddenly lunged forwards. I came off, out of the new no-horse-can-throw-me poley saddle and Ty took off in a mad panic down the furrows of sugarcane. My left arm felt funny but Ty's hasty runaway flight more than worried me. 'He'll be right,' Tom tried to reassure me. 'He'll come back to his mate.' I wasn't too sure about the 'mate' bit. The two horses had only just met but, as suddenly as it had started, the storm abruptly disappeared and Ty was standing beside the shed whinnying disconsolately. I raced out and caught him. He had a few shallow scratches, probably from the barb wire of the cocky's gate, but no real harm done. The farmer's cane didn't look unrecoverably trampled and Ty had neither broken a rein nor lost one of my stirrups. My luck was in.

Tom had to help me mount. Ty was a tall horse and my left arm felt pretty useless. 'Broken,' he said. 'No', I replied. 'I can use my fingers.' He accepted that without comment and we rode back to Molly and Vin's, getting there before dark. Mort was there. He was pleased that we'd got out of the storm relatively unscathed and more pleased when Tom said he'd take Ty but he thought I should have my arm 'seen to'. I disagreed. I was off duty until one the next day and had no intention of returning early. My arm kept up its painful ache through the night and I ended up curling in beside Molly in the big double bed.

Next day, Mort appeared in his ute. He just 'happened' to be passing and could drive me to the hospital. My bike could go in the back. Goodbyes were said and Molly made me promise to get my arm seen to. Back at the quarters, my mates didn't like the look of my arm, either. Any doubts I'd had as to the wisdom of getting it 'seen to' disappeared when I had trouble getting the swollen arm into my uniform sleeve. To make sure I wouldn't chicken out, one of my mates was delegated to escort me to Outpatients before I was due in the wards. Luckily, friend Humph was on duty. 'Riding bloody horses', he commented. 'Yes,' I agreed. 'Better not tell Matron that. You fell down the steps.' He was gently touching my arm, swollen and black and blue with bruising. 'Where does it hurt?' 'Everywhere.' He gave me a professional look and a slight frown as if to say 'be more explicit' but what he did say was , 'It's a bad break.' I was about to wiggle my fingers to prove it wasn't when he took my fingers in a firm but gentle grip. 'We're taking bones, not tendons.' So much for my erroneous folkloric belief.

'We'll x-ray it.'

My mate was dispatched to the ward to tell them that I'd fallen down the steps and hurt my arm. The x-ray showed a fractured wrist-bone and a small piece splintered off one of the long forearm bones at my elbow. No wonder I couldn't pinpoint where it hurt. Humph said that there'd have to be an open reduction. Dr. Scott would operate. He'd open up at the elbow and remove the bone splinter. The wrist would heal just by restricting movement. As I was not yet twenty-one, I'd have to get my parents' consent for the anaesthetic. In the meantime, I was to be admitted to sickbay and starved, ready for the op. the next day.

Cyclone to the Rescue

Just as the lightning bolt that initiated the action was unexpected, so was the cyclone that hit Cooktown. All communications were 'out'. My parents couldn't be contacted. After a couple of days in sickbay with my arm strapped to a padded splint, Dr. Scott and Humph came for a second look. After prodding below my elbow, Dr. Scott thought that the splinter was beginning to fuse back to the bone. I could be discharged. However, there was a 'but'. I had to have my arm restrained in a 'cuff and collar'. When the swelling reduced, it would be plastered. In the meantime, I couldn't go back to the wards. I was on three weeks sick leave. My wrist was encircled with a padded 'cuff' and a small sling elevated my arm to a fairly comfortable position with my cuffed hand up near my throat. Then came the scary part. I was to report to Matron. As I left, Humph stage-whispered, 'fell down the steps,' so I knew what to expect.

As to be expected, Matron wasn't pleased. She was one nurse down. 'How did it happen, Nurse?' she asked through disapproving lips.

'I fell down the steps, Matron.' I had it off pat. I'd been practising mentally.

'Going on or off duty, Nurse?'

I hadn't expected that.

'At a friend's place on my day off, Matron.'

Teddy wasn't pleased when I recounted the interview. Matron was giving me the chance of putting in for compo. Cooktown was still incommunicado. I went out to Molly's and from there arranged to go out to Bessie at Barcoola.

A Happy Enforced Holiday

Fortunately, being on sick leave, I had some sick pay to fall back on. Dad wrote to me regularly and, when he could, sent me a pound ($2) note. It helped pay the twenty-six pounds ($52) my lovely new saddle had cost me. Vin lent me some money to make the purchase and I had just about paid him back. There was a little left in my betting fund so I was fairly confident when I boarded the first train that would take me to Brisbane to catch the others to Roma and to Injune. Bess drove into town to meet me. She knew how I really broke my arm and, though she didn't altogether approve of girls riding thoroughbred stallions, was rather sympathetic. On the drive back to Barcoola she told me about this superlative racehorse she had seen on the Western Circuit and fallen in love with . Beautiful conformation and temperament. He could be for sale. The owners hadn't quite made up their minds about selling but, if they did, she had first offer. She didn't refuse when he did come on the market and he became her wonder-horse, Gallant.

It was good to see some of the old horses that I knew still looking well. The season had been reasonable and the stock looked good, though with woolly sheep it was harder for me to judge their condition. Bess took me for a few short rides with her to check waters and some newly-dropped lambs but insisted on opening and shutting the gates herself. It took me too long to dismount and to clamber on again but I did get to turn the forge for Bert with my good hand and made myself a little bit useful. Bert was training a couple of up-and-coming dogs for a sheepdog trial and possible sale, so I watched, tried to learn a few pointers, and did simple chores to help out. The time passed far too quickly. Happily I did not know that it was to be the last time I would ever see Bert.

Back again at Bundaberg I had a couple of days with Molly before reporting back to Out Patients. The swelling in my arm had reduced much as Humph had forecast and it was time to have a plaster applied. As I couldn't go back into the wards with a plaster, I was to take my annual leave. Humph suggested to the Out Patient's sister that, as I was going off to Cooktown and beyond, a good heavy-duty plaster would be in order. They took him at his word and must've used double the usual amount of plaster of Paris. One night, camped out at Butcher's Hill, I rolled over swinging my arm and inadvertently clocked Ruth, in her swag next to me. She claimed I hit her head and could have knocked her out but I don't think I was that accurate. Maybe she exaggerated just a little bit.

With the Wet Season hanging on, I was doubtful when I stepped off the launch in Cooktown, if I'd be able to make it out to Butcher's Hill. Dad said that they hadn't had a mail there since before Christmas. With only packhorse mails it was too dangerous to cross the flooded, unbridged rivers. One of my old riding mates, Micky Finn, lost his dad by drowning. He was the Bloomfield mailman and a rogue current took his life. The rule was, or so I was told, not to go in water over knee-pad deep. Deeper than that, a horse would be unable to keep its footing but I personally thought that knee-pad height was a bit on the dangerous side. One day Dad came home with good news for me. The weather looked as if the heavy rain was over and Norman was planning to do a mail trip that week. If the weather held, as he was sure it would, he'd do a second trip a week later with the accumulated back-log. He could take me out and back if it suited. It sounded good to me and Dad arranged for a lift to Helenvale for me with one of the Doolan brothers in their ex-Army jeep. They mined tin at Rossville, out from Helenvale and had come in for supplies. Mrs. Watkin seemed pleased to see me again and Norman and I had no trouble on our ride to Butcher's Hill.

Quick Sand

A week wasn't long enough, of course, but it proved to be ample time for me to, typically, get myself into a rather ticklish situation. We had come to Ninda Creek and the Boss, followed closely by Jack and Ruth were making heavy going of ploughing through the crossing. The water wasn't that deep, or that strong. Unfortunately, I thought I heard the different beat of Banfield's drum and decided to cross by myself just below them. Before anyone realised what I had in mind, Flame began first to sink and then frantically struggle and plunge to get her equilibrium. Jack, having reached the other side, jumped off his horse and rushed in to grab Flame's bridle. After a few hectic moments, we managed to free ourselves from the weird underwater force and reach the bank safely, Flame's sides heaving and my heart thumping. The Boss was not amused, though the other two, once I was rescued, almost laughed their heads off. Ninda Creek was renowned for its quicksand and everyone (except me) knew that the only way to deal with the treachery of quicksand was to go slowly, one behind the other, each horse's hoofs helping to compact the shifting sand for the ones that followed. I had wet sand most uncomfortably in my boots and in my saddlebag. Stopping later to boil-up, I found I had sand in my sandwiches as well and some had sneaked in under my heavy-duty plaster to make its presence felt for days. There were enough grains left there to puzzle the Outpatients' staff when my heavy-duty plaster was later exchanged for a more normal, light-weight one. I gained my quicksand experience without major problems and Ruth and Jack bestowed a nick-name, Ninda, on me as a reminder. I quite liked it and when I later wrote for R.M.Williams' *Hoofs and Horns*, Ninda was my nom de plume.

End of an Era

The time too quickly passed and it was with mixed feelings that, one evening Ruth and I saw Norman riding up through the paddock from Boggy Creek. Next morning, with promises to come and visit again, Norman and I left with the out-going mail and reached Helenvale in good time. Mrs. Watkin wanted to go in to Cooktown so she managed to get a lift in for us both the next day. She was going to stay with a friend who owned the Commercial (now Cooktown) Hotel for a few days.

My riding mates had gone back to their usual jobs. I didn't see Alan but Royce called in at the Court House to get some paperwork under control while I was there with Dad. I was more than a bit concerned about my father. He seemed to have lost some of his boundless zest for life. Mum said it could be 'gall bladder trouble' and was angling for a transfer further south where all the medical facilities were more readily available. Dad gave me a message from Miss Eichorn. Caroline had something for me. I was wondering what other advice she had to impart and left on Dad's bike with rather mixed feelings. If her home had been a bit down-market before, it now resembled an uncared-for rubbish dump. She indicated my customary deck-chair while she went to get me a drink. The deck-chair and piles of newspapers and bottles were still there but the cyclone had moved several of the sheets of roofing iron. To counteract the lack of cover, Caroline had laid a sheet of iron, weighted-down at either end, on the supporting piles of newspaper to shelter the visitors' chair. Huddled there, I felt a bit like a possum in a hollow tree. Caroline told me of the problems she was having getting financiers interested in backing her beloved proposal for the cannery and jam, pickle and chutney factory. The cyclone had long-reaching effects. I agreed with all she had to say and tried to answer her questions about doctors and nurses while privately thinking how Humph would've enjoyed this outing.

Miss Eichorn's Gift

As I was ready to leave, Caroline got a chair to get down my gift from her, a Christmas cake. It was suspended in a kerosene tin bucket under the few remaining sheets of the verandah roof. As she took out the cake in its calico wrapping I automatically took a step back. It was covered with blue mould. The bucket had been a very, very, wet storage place.

'Don't worry,' comforted Caroline, pushing it into my reluctant hands. 'It's only the wrapping. The cake's all right. I put rum in it.'

I thanked her and pedalled off promising to give my father her very best wishes.

As I drew level with the Commercial, I saw my friend Mrs. Watkin and decided to show her my present. She couldn't stop laughing but took the messy thing from me with a secretive, 'Come on. Follow me.'

We went upstairs to where our mutual friend, Tom Foster, in from Starcke for a few days, had a room. Fortunately for Mrs. Watkin's scheme, though perhaps not for Tom, he wasn't there. She stripped his bed and remade it, short-sheeting the top sheet in a way that a sleep-seeker's feet would be blocked half way down the bed. At this fold she deposited the mouldy cake, camouflaging its lumpy outline under the bed quilt as best she could. I think it achieved the effect she desired as, over fifty years later, Tom still remembers the occasion. 'Typical Kathleen.' Ruth's sister Joyce also remembers a similar experience when Mrs. Watkins short-sheeted both girls' beds at Helenvale with a couple of eggs in the doubled-back sheet. I was lucky that she didn't play the same prank on me. Perhaps she did, the nights I stayed there but I was too tired to notice.

It was hard to say goodbye to Dad and to go so far away. He did not look at all like his usual cheerful self. Mum spoke of a couple of vacancies that were coming up and for which she hoped Dad would apply. One was for a Police Magistrate at Kingaroy.

Back at Bundy, a visit to Outpatients was the first priority. Dr. Scott and Humph were pleased with the way the bones had knitted but both recommended the replacement of the heavy plaster by a lightweight one for another few weeks. I could go back on duty, not in the wards but helping the physio and with X-rays and plasters in Outpatients. When the heavy plaster (and its remaining sand) was removed my arm was a most repulsive white with touches of a slimey green. With suntanned fingers, it looked rather weird and I wasn't sorry to see a plaster go on over it. The physio noticed, too, that .I didn't have full movement in my wrist and worked on it before the plaster was applied. She also passed on a very good tip that I've since relayed to others in a similar situation. This was that every time I came to a door knob, I was to use my left hand to activate the knob whether I needed to use the door or not. I heeded the advice and was sure that it helped restore the movement. Molly had borrowed a violin for me to play hill-billy songs for Vin. At first I couldn't rotate my hand enough to grasp the neck of the violin. By putting the neck between thumb and forefinger of my left hand and using the violin itself as a lever, I could persuade my wrist to oblige and that speeded recovery up as well.

The year brought changes at the hospital. Teddy and Audrey having served their extra time, gained their registration and their sisters' veils and left. Newcomers included two senior nurses experienced in other branches of nursing. They'd trained at the Mental Hospital at Goodna but, like Teddy and Audrey, needed wider experience to gain their Registered General Nursing status. One, Shuttie, with whom I worked on several occasions, went on further when she'd completed the necessary General training. She took up Maternal and Child Welfare, advising new mothers on the care of babies and other small children. In that capacity, I met her again some years later when she worked on a circuit from Cairns to Thursday Island and taking in Cooktown. It was great to see her again.

It was about this time that Matron sent for me and one of the other nurses. My plaster had been removed and I was back in the wards again (and doing a bit of roadwork on the side for Tom). The two of us were the only trainees at Bundaberg General who had passed Senior (Year 12) and qualified for matriculation to University. Matron took our educational particulars but after another couple of calls to her office, we heard no more. That was over fifty years ago and, looking back, I sometimes wonder if that was the start of the movement to upgrade nursing training to a university course rather than just hands-on hospital experience.

My concern about Dad's health was sadly justified. He received the promotion and transfer to Kingaroy where he had his gall bladder removed. I was able to visit them for my holidays. Apart from my father's deteriorating health, everything looked fine. They had rented a comfortable home, renewed some old friendships and made many more, but I could see that Dad had to call up a lot of effort to display his usual enthusiasm and zest for life. I met his young doctor and thought that he was a bit like Humph in the way he took his patient's problems to heart. The gall bladder operation was a success as far as the actual operation went, but the doctor was not at all convinced that it was the root of the problem. He arranged for further wide-ranging tests and the verdict was bad. Dad had cancer of the liver and it was quickly spreading via his lymph glands to other parts of his body. The young doctor thought it may have begun as far back as Dad's malaria relapse in Tully.

There was no point in Dad applying for sick leave. He resigned. Mum sorted out their belongings, sold some and kept what she valued most and put it in storage. Dad commenced a long stay, mostly spent in hospitals, in Brisbane where his older widowed sister, Mag, was living. Jean had completed her pharmacy training and had started off overseas to take up her old American friend's offer of relieving work in Indiana. New Zealand was her first, and for many years her permanent, stop. She fell in love and was to be married. We still hoped that Dr. O's diagnosis might be wrong. Besides being brilliant, he was also rather young. Our fingers were crossed. Jean and her Les were planning their wedding to fit in with a suggested trip to New Zealand by Mum and Dad. It wasn't to be. Dr. O's clinical conclusion was accurate. Dad's days were numbered and his strength and vigour declined rapidly under our anxious eyes. Jean and Les were married on August 25th 1950, Dad's 54th birthday. I managed to get down to Brisbane to be with my parents but I don't think the double import of the day registered with Dad at all. I went back to Bundaberg knowing that I wouldn't have my beloved Dad for much longer.

Aunt Mag, with whom Mum was staying when she wasn't at Dad's bedside, agreed that Mum should prepare herself for the worst and to make arrangements to move on, when the sad time came, to her own sisters in Sydney. I agreed that it was the only way to go. Back at Bundaberg most of my friends had either moved on or were ready to go after the results of our finals exam at the end of the year. In October I was rostered to take my place as 'scout', the junior nurse, in Theatre, something we all looked forward to as the high point of our training. With Theatre accomplished, and with finals out of the way, it was only left for me to do my 'time'. Four years would be up in March and I'd be Sister Waddell. It was a hard decision to make but I couldn't leave Mum to cope with Dad's failing health on her own.

Sister was sympathetic and organised six days off for me by rostering my normal two days off from the first week to be followed immediately by the two days off from the next week. We worked without overtime payment but there was a clause that said that if we worked on a public holiday of the importance of Christmas or Labor Day we were entitled to another day off, but at no pay. Few nurses took advantage of this, but luckily, I had worked on those two days and Sister added them to the four I was already due. I was ever so grateful for Sister's kindly act and arrived at the hospital in time to have two days with my father who was in terrible pain all the while despite his four-hourly morphine. He died on the second day of October, my twentieth birthday.

Like me, Aunt Mag was very worried about Mum. She and Dad had known each other all their lives and he had been her first 'serious' boyfriend. They'd been married so happily for over twenty-five years and now her life and her future lay in tatters. This became very apparent when she went missing one evening and Aunt and I found her walking along the bank of the Brisbane River. Her beloved Jack was calling her.

Queensland Nurse No Longer

I hurried back to Bundaberg and put in my resignation. Aunt Mag was helping Mum make arrangements to move to her sister in Sydney and I felt that I must go with her. It seemed so unfair that I was just rostered for Theatre and that I'd soon be finished training but there was no alternative. Matron wasn't so keen on the idea and offered me six months special leave but I was in no condition to think straight. Mum's riverside walk and her sad bereavement were uppermost in my thoughts. Besides, as junior of my year, by the time I returned after six months, all my old mates would have gone. I thanked Matron but stuck to my decision to resign. I packed what clothes I needed and stashed what was left together with my riding gear at Tom's stables. I had doubts about leaving my shoe box of Dad's letters, my photo albums and show ribbons. I clung to the box of letters until the last moment. Tom said he'd send them all down as soon as I had a permanent address and I clutched that straw and thanked him, caught the train to Brisbane and joined my mother on our way to Sydney.

Once we were settled in, Mum recovered from her badly-depressed state and feeling that I could now leave her, I went to stay with a cousin, older than I was, with a husband and two young sons. We got on exceptionally well. She lived not far from the local hospital so, with her assistance, I arranged for an appointment with the Sister in Charge, hoping that they'd take me on and I could complete my training there. I had my Queensland transfer papers which stated the length of time I had trained and the examinations passed, so felt quite confident. I wouldn't even mind if they'd allowed for the six weeks probation period. I certainly wasn't prepared when Sister told me that Queensland training wasn't accepted in N.S.W. If I'd passed my finals, completed my time and received my registration, it would have been a different matter. As a Sister I could get a job anywhere in Australia and in most countries overseas. Probably Matron knew all that and thought that I did, too.

My cousin Phyl, who had gone with me, rallied to the occasion. When we returned to her place and sat with cups of steaming nerve-settling tea in front of us, she consulted the daily newspaper and found a vacancy for nurses at a private hospital on the north shore. It was on the railway, she said, so it'd be no trouble getting to work She rang the number, gave my particulars and was told that I could start work there the next morning at nine. Uniforms would be provided. It was quite exciting to get off at the station and follow the map Phyl had drawn to the hospital. It was a nursing home rather than a hospital and was set in the most beautiful tree-shaded grounds. The main building had been one of the original 'stately homes' and was really superb. I hurried in with an escort provided at reception to be given two uniforms and shown a locker that would be for my use. The other nurse, a Sister wearing her veil, handed me a voile square. 'Put it on'.

'But,but,but...' I stammered. 'I told them at the desk. I didn't finish my training.'

'This hospital employs only trained staff. Put it on.'

I was helpless but she suited action to her words and pinned the once-coveted veil onto my head. 'You'll be addressed as Sister'.

She took me to a ward full of elderly women patients, introduced me and left. Where did I start? Apparently, it was time for medications so I went around with another Sister, handing out an assortment of pills, including, I recognised, quite a few sedatives. The patients were mostly bed-ridden though a few were in chairs on the long, ferny verandah. One woman was shaking so badly with Parkinson's she could barely get the tablets to her mouth, let alone the glass of water. I stood back, expecting the other Sister to help her. She didn't.

It didn't take long for me to realise that, despite the much better pay, this wasn't the job for me. In Queensland's free Public Hospital system the standard of care was infinitely higher. My thoughts returned repeatedly to Deputy Matron when I was refused a clean draw-sheet for an incontinent patient. 'We change the draw-sheets daily and the bed sheets on Mondays', I was told. In the meantime, patients were left to lie on wet and sometimes soiled sheets. Bed- sores were not at all rare and I wondered how a little bit of metho and a few minutes for a wash and a back-rub could be considered an unnecessary expense. There were none of the feeding cups I was familiar with, relatively spill-free and with a drinking spout. Shaky hands spilt hot and cold drinks whenever they were provided. Similarly, no assistance was provided to patients who found difficulty in feeding themselves. Deputy Matron would have had the mother of all fits could she see it.

My enthusiasm in getting a job all too quickly evaporated. A sympathetic fellow 'Sister' took me aside one day.

'If you want to leave, wait until payday. Collect your pay and don't come back. If you tell them you're going, they'll make you give four weeks' notice.'

I took her advice.

Phyl's husband found the next job, also on the north-side commuter line, a nurse but not for looking after humans. A vet. was advertising for a nurse 'with experience with animals'. I phoned and got the job. It was a combined practice both for small and for large animals. For the first fortnight I worked for the vet. treating cats, dogs and budgies. It was constant work and interesting. Then I was moved to the large animal practice. The second vet. held positions with the big racing and trotting clubs and a lot of the work entailed travelling out to various stables. I was hooked. Maybe this was the job for me. A small second thought crept in. Would it be too late to go to Uni. and do Vet. Science? Would they accept a Queensland matriculation?

My dreams were immediately shattered when my Boss began pulling up off the road on our way back from the studs or stables we'd been visiting and attempted to study human anatomy on me. Pay-day was coming up. I managed to dodge the wandering hands until pay-day when his wife gave me my cheque. Did I detect a doubting, disapproving look? Following my strategy at the nursing home, I didn't turn up for work the following Monday and an ad. for a new Vet. nurse duly appeared in the paper. My next job was a rather strange one, comptometer operator at the Staff Pay Office at David Jones. I didn't know what a comptometer looked like, let alone what you were expected to do with it.

'You'll learn,' said Phyl and I was encouraged by her cousinly faith in me.

It was a pleasant work-place and everyone was very helpful. I soon became, if not the 'competent' comptometrist asked for in the ad., at least a reasonably useful one. To get to work, I had a very enjoyable ferry ride and a then quick walk to David Jones with another walk back to the harbour side after work. I enjoyed the ferry rides despite shivering apprehensively when shown where the Japanese mini-subs had lurked in the war and where the *Kuttabul* had been sunk. Everyone was friendly but I had come to the conclusion that city life, in the long term, was definitely not for me. Mum was with her eldest sister, Jean, at Dee Why. I went to visit when I could but I must confess I spent most of my time with Aunt Jean's son Peter and his girl friend, Joy, later to become his wife. We spent some time on the beach but they were rabid jazz fans and played the old vinyl 78s of Louis Armstrong, Fats Waller and other Dixieland bands almost non-stop. Thanks to them, I became a life-long trad. Jazz enthusiast.

The truth was, I suppose, that I missed my horses. I'd written to Tom asking him to send down Dad's letters, my photos and ribbons. I enclosed money for postage but received no reply. Molly wrote that she'd go round to see him, package up my letters and things and take my riding gear to her place. I eagerly awaited the card to say that there was a parcel for me at the Post Office but, instead, another letter came from Molly. She'd been around to the stable to find that Tom had sold all 'his' gear and gone to New Zealand to train trotters. I guess my precious memorabilia had no commercial value and was trashed. It looked as if Teddy had been right about those shifty eyes.

A New Job Offer

D.J's was a good place to work but ... I decided that with Mum settled in with her family, there was no need for me to be in Sydney, or even in N.S.W.. I dug out my old transfer form and wrote a letter to the hospital at Goondiwindi to see if they had a vacancy. I was heading up to post it when I picked up a letter for me in Phyl's letterbox at the gate. It was from Ruth. She was in trouble. Either

I came up and kept her company in the mustering camp or she had to go away nursing. Her Dad would pay me wages and would be pleased if I could come.

I changed my mind about transferring to Goondiwindi and went back inside the house with Phyl's mail to write Ruth a reply. And that is how I went back to Butcher's Hill.

Joyce had finished her training, married a Peninsula cattleman's son and moved out with him to a manager's job on another property. This time, Ruth's brother Bill was home. I'd just missed him on my last visit. He'd left for Lakefield the week before but now his father had sold his share in Lakefield to his partner and Bill had returned home to run the stock camp. With him had come his foster-brother Paddy, one of the three Aboriginal children his parents had reared, and Paddy's partner, Leo – Leah, really. Leo came from tribe near Cooktown. She and another Aboriginal man were the only two survivors of a tribe wiped out by European–introduced diseases including syphilis. Leo thought syphilis had been the cause of her mother's early death and possibly she, too, was affected. Though she whole-heartedly longed for a child she never had one and when she died it was from an 'enlarged heart', an end-result of syphilis.

The sexes were evenly represented in the Boss's mustering plant. Ruth, Leo and me plus Bill, Paddy and Edwin Gostelow who became a highly-valued friend for life. Edwin had been working with Bill and returned to Butcher's Hill when he came home. Jack was still with us but only for a few months. Bill's mother felt the need to retire from the constant grind of the station. She was from the Atherton Tableland and, when told of a good dairy farm for sale near Malanda at a reasonable price, she and the Boss had a look and bought it. Jack would go over to help her with the heavy work but if we could keep the station going in its usual orderly fashion, the Boss would join her. The road had just been pushed through from Mt. Carbine out from Mareeba, to Cooktown. We loaded all the things Mrs. Wallace wanted to take with her on the station's new Dodge truck and Jack drove her to her new home.

Life in the mustering camp was great but trying to fit it in with the usual station cooking such as breadmaking wasn't quite as fulfilling. The yeast bottle, a big beer bottle with a cork tied down with string, was the precursor of the more modern yeasts and needed feeding daily much like the old-time ginger beer plant, the starter for celebratory ginger beers. We were told different ways to liven up a rather lifeless yeast bottle, a sultana or two, a bit of the water rice was cooked in and, at times, these did work. On other occasions the additions had differing effects ranging from doing absolutely nothing to invigorate the yeast to over-prescribing and popping the yeast bottle corks. On one thankfully rare occasion our ministrations acted like dynamite and blew-up the yeast bottle. We managed somehow. Ivy Elmes was living at Springvale then and, in an emergency, could be relied on to help out with a new yeast starter.

I Meet Ruth's Brother

Bill was all my Cooktown mates had told me. Genuinely kind-hearted and a wizard with horses, cattle and dogs. He could get them to do anything he wanted and made it look as if they enjoyed co-operating with him as well. He seemed a lot like my Dad but lacked Dad's social skills. He was rather shy, especially with the 'opposite sex'. Ruth, with her usual sense of fun, bet me one of her less-favoured horses that I couldn't get Bill to kiss me within four weeks of when we met. I totally lacked Ruth's talent for flirtation. Boys, as a romantic subject, hadn't interested me. As mates doing interesting and exciting things, well, that was different. With all this on my mind, I was more than a little surprised when, about a week after the expiry of Ruth's deadline, Bill rode up close to me as we were coming in to camp one evening, put his arm on my shoulder and gave me a quick kiss on the cheek. I was in love.

Of course, Ruth with her eagle eye, soon found out what was brewing and began making plans.

'Get married at Laura Races time. Everyone will be there.'

Bill and I hadn't talked marriage. I was still under twenty-one and would have to get permission from my parent to take that important step. Very secretly Bill wrote the necessary letter and slipped it to Norman to post.

At the Malanda farm, Mrs. Wallace had got wind of the romance and stepped in suggesting a quiet family wedding at her farmhouse. She and my mother got their heads together and arranged it all. The 'permission' wasn't legally necessary. I had turned twenty-one about two months earlier.

On the few occasions that Ruth and I visited the bar at the Laura pub, a rather puzzling thing would happen. Sweatie, an old World War 1 digger, would come up to us at the soft-drink end of the bar, and start to ask me something. His drinking companions would immediately shut him up before he could get the question out. A couple of years later when I called at the bar and found Sweatie alone there, he took advantage of the encounter to blurt out the question that had been worrying him.

'Who did the askin'?' He had known Bill for many years.

No one. We just decided that we were right for each other. No questions were asked and no answers needed to be given. Almost fifty years of very worthwhile life were spent together. We were good mates.

About the Author

Lennie Wallace has been writing since an early age though the first editions were only of two copies, typed with a carbon paper back-up by her father. Her first paid submission was for a short story in the *Brisbane Telegraph* while she was a boarder at Brisbane Girls Grammar School and had run out of pocketmoney. The second submission was not successful.

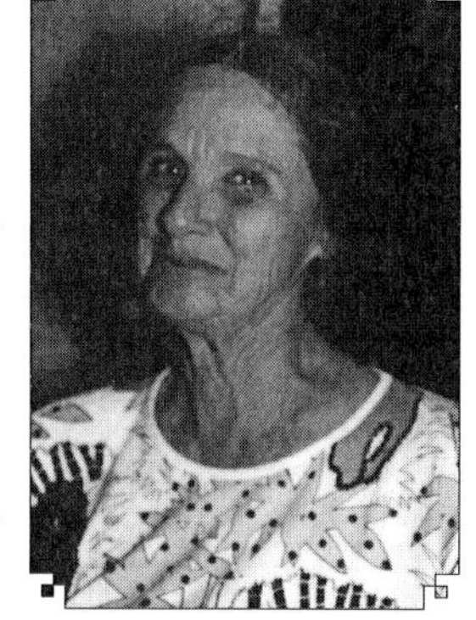

At R.M. Williams' request, she began writing bush verse, articles, stories and Peninsula Notes for *Hoofs and Horns.* At about the same time she sold two articles and several pars to the old *Sydney Bulletin* magazine and current women's magazines.

Her first book *Leaves from the Peninsula* was published by Pinevale Publications in 1990. A fellow *Hoofs and Horns* writer suggested that she submit it to Central Queensland University Press & Old Silvertail's Outback Books, Rockhampton, for re-publishing. As a result it was re-issued as *Bow Waves in the Bull Dust* in 1996. It was followed by:

Bitten by the Bull Bug	1997
Dad and Joey in Possum Gully	1999
Nomads of the 19th Century Goldfields	2000
Battlers of Butcher's Hill	2002
Cape York Peninsula: A History of Unlauded Heroes	2004

Also a short story writer, she has won or placed in various Queensland short story competitions and has had stories included in *L.I.N.Q. Vol 19 No 1* (1992), *The Cooktown Collection* (1997), *Pretty to Watch with a Shovel* (Ashgrove Writers, 2003), *Fifty Flies Since Smoko* (Remote Writers, Cairns, 1992, 2001) and *Voices from Elsewhere* (Rural Women Writers Group, 1994, 1995).

She has also had bush verse published in *Hoofs and Horns, N.Q.R.*, the *Bronze Swagman (Winton) Collection* and in *A Thousand Campfires* (Royal Agricultural Society of Victoria). Other verse was printed in *Micropress* (Yates).

Books by
Lennie Wallace

Bow Waves in the Bull Dust

Bitten by the Bull Bug

Nomads of the 19th Century Queensland Goldfields

The Battlers of Butchers Hill

Cape York Peninsula

From Nanango to Cooktown